Your *Possible* Life

How to Build the Life of Your Dreams

KATHY MURPHY, PhD

To Michael,
For all your unending support, unwavering loyalty, and
undying love, thank you for making my best life possible.

Published by Advantage, Charleston, South Carolina.
Member of Advantage Media Group.

ADVANTAGE is a registered trademark and the Advantage colophon is a trademark of Advantage Media Group, Inc.

Printed in the United States of America.

ISBN: 978-1-59932-243-8
LCCN: 2011902202

Advantage Media Group is proud to be a part of the Tree Neutral® program. Tree Neutral offsets the number of trees consumed in the production and printing of this book by taking proactive steps such as planting trees in direct proportion to the number of trees used to print books. To learn more about Tree Neutral, please visit **www.treeneutral.com**. To learn more about Advantage's commitment to being a responsible steward of the environment, please visit **www.advantagefamily.com/green**

Advantage Media Group is a leading publisher of business, motivation, and self-help authors. Do you have a manuscript or book idea that you would like to have considered for publication? Please visit **www.amgbook.com** or call **1.866.775.1696**

Contents

Design Sheets

PART I

Introduction

"I have heard it all my life...

A voice calling a name I recognized as my own.

Saying: Remember who you truly are

And let this knowing take you home."

- Oriah Mountain Dreamer

I

M any years ago, I bought a driftwood-framed picture of a little beach house sitting behind the dunes of a gentle, glistening beach. I hung this picture in my office and every day I would gaze upon it and visualize myself in this dreamy cottage.

This sweet house by the sea came to represent all the things that I longed for in my life; things like simplicity, tranquility, nature (specifically the sea), solitude, serenity, peace and quiet...you get the picture. Everything about this house felt safe and familiar, everything about it felt true about me. This beautiful vision spoke to me. It started calling my name. And it started calling me home, back to myself and to how I longed to live my life.

Where do you live? Not your address, not the physical place you eat and sleep, but the place within you that knows your heart's longings and calls you home?

We're all trying to find home, searching for that place that is the truest and deepest expression of our potential. We are looking for the life of our dreams. Not the life that our mother and father wanted for us, not the life that we wind up with through a series of defaults and bad choices, but the life that is uniquely programmed into our DNA, the life that is rightfully meant to be ours.

We hear a lot of talk today that you can have anything that you can dream. That's both true and not true, and we all know it. We all know there are certain things we will never be. I will never be President of the United States or run a giant multi-national corporation. Not because of my age, or because I have no political or business background or support, or any other external limitations - those kind of obstacles can be overcome. I will never be President or CEO because it is not now and never has been in my longings or desires, or in my creative, spiritually-infused, DNA. These are simply not goals that naturally call my name. And if I get seduced (as we all do) into following a dream fueled by the ego or others' persuasions—well, we all know that these are the dreams that tend to fail. *I suggest that these are not the true dreams of your life.*

I believe that our truest dreams, the ones that are encoded into our DNA, come loaded with information about who we really are, what we really want, and the life of which we are capable. These are the dreams that lead us to happiness, fulfillment, and satisfaction. We want to listen for this inner wisdom and let it guide our lives.

There are many dreams that visit me in the night and stretch out before me saying, "Come and follow me." These are the deep longings and desires that come from my inner loving voice of wisdom and guidance. This is the voice that told me to write this book. Writing a book required a big leap of faith for me. But, unlike being president, this is a dream that calls my name, one for which I believe I have potential and possibility. It's a big dream, so it pushes me to grow. We all have many beautiful, tremendous, unique gifts and potentials that are naturally ours. Let's forget trying to be something that we aren't.

If I learn to listen for my inner loving voice, if I have the courage to step out and into these dreams, if I am willing to believe, and if I am willing to go through the building process it takes, I will end up in the home — the life — I've always dreamed of.

We've grown to be skeptical about undertaking yet another program that promises us that we can have the life of our dreams because, unfortunately, a lot of our best efforts have gone wrong. We don't want to be hurt or disappointed, or to fail yet again. Instead, to improve our chances for success, I suggest we focus on becoming clear about who we really are, uncovering our truest talents and deepest longings, and then and only then, begin to build a life on this foundation.

This life design process is about helping you ask and answer the powerful questions of your life, to reveal who you really are and what you really want, and then to apply this knowledge to point you to your next possible steps. My job is to guide you on your journey back to yourself. Your job is to learn the tools that are available to help you access your inner wisdom, activate your personal power, and to begin to build the life of your dreams.

I encourage you to take this journey. It's worth the effort. When you are clear about who you are and what you want from your deepest, truest level, and when you begin making choices and acting on this self knowledge and awareness, you will arrive at a place you will recognize, finally, as home.

Can you hear the voice that calls your name?
Can you hear the voice that says,
"Remember who you really are and what you really want?"
And, if you can hear it, do you listen?

POWERFUL QUESTION:

What dreams come to you in the middle of the night and call your name.... calling you back home to yourself?

PART II

Your Possible Life

This is an invitation to stop

To stop and take some time

To consider your life,

Who you are,

What you want,

And what your possibilities are...

II

Have you ever awakened in the middle of the night with the scary thought—"Wait a minute. This is not the life I am supposed to be living!" You try to shrug it off, but the thought lingers, and it haunts you—because you know it's true. There's no escaping or denying it any longer. You know, deep down inside, that you are not living in a way that expresses who you really are. You are not at home in your own life.

For some of us, it's not a new thought. We've heard an inner call to live our lives differently for a long time. Sometimes it's a call for a big dream like world peace, or maybe it's just a little call for working on our own daily peace. Maybe the call comes as a new career or a divorce. Maybe the call is the awareness that we are not living the lifestyle we want—a lifestyle that includes exercise, fresh air, good eating patterns and choices, or turning off the TV and getting a full night's sleep. For some of us, we know we are not being in our relationships the way that we want. Or we are not doing work that inspires and motivates us. Maybe we aren't financially responsible, or intellectually and creatively stimulated. Most of us feel we are not living like the spiritual beings that we know ourselves to be. Yet all of these things are possible for each of us and they will transform our lives. And, step by step, they will take us home.

Your Possible Life is the life design model that I developed for my own life, and have gone on to teach to thousands of people, in my private practice, at conferences, and at retreats. This book is for anyone who's ready to step off the treadmill, to go on an inner journey of self-rediscovery, and to get conscious and active about how you are living your life. This work will help you get reacquainted with who you really are, what you really want, and your true possibilities for a more fulfilling life. Like Dorothy in *The Wizard of Oz*, we all just want to get home. Luckily, like Dorothy, we all have the power within to get us there.

"How we spend our days is, of course, how we spend our lives."
— **ANNIE DILLARD**

POWERFUL QUESTION:

Is how you are spending your days a reflection
of the life you want to be living?

*"We begin to find
and become ourselves
when we notice how
we already are...
who we are truly, entirely,
wildly, messily and marvelously,
who we were born to be."*

– ANNE LAMONT

Your One True Life

There's an old joke about a woman who wanted a great outfit like the ones she'd seen on her friends and celebrities. One day she saw just the right dress in a store window and went in to try it on. But it didn't quite fit. The right sleeve was a little long - but the sales clerk said "That's okay, just hold your shoulder up a little." When she did that, the left shoulder hitched up. The clerk said, "That's okay, just sorta push that back, like so." When she did, the bottom of the skirt twisted, so she twisted her body just so. And the sales clerk said, "There, that's fine, now it fits." The woman left the store and was walking down the street when a couple passed. The man said, "Honey, did you see that woman? Poor thing, did you see the anguish she was in? His wife said, "Yeah, but isn't that a great dress?"

How many of us are walking around in lives that don't fit? Lives that require us to contort and distort everything that's real about us, to make them work? Oh, we may look pretty good on the outside, but it doesn't match up with what we are feeling on the inside at all.

We aren't experiencing a smooth fit between our inner and our outer selves. Somehow, we've ended up living life according to someone else's values and ideas. We've designed our lives based on what our parents, teachers, society, friends, or employers wanted. Or we've ended up living our lives by default—because of bad choices, lack of choices, or simply not making a choice. However we got here, we're in a life that doesn't fit.

While some of us are confused and unsure about what it would take to truly bring us happiness, satisfaction, and alignment, most of us really already know. Even so, we don't act on it. Days go by, weeks go by, sometimes even years go by, and we don't make the desired shifts. Then we wake up one day (or in the middle of the night) and we wonder, "How in the world did I get here?" But by this time we feel so mired in our habits and patterns that change feels impossible and over-whelming. So we just keep on. We don't know what else to do.

But you do know — and you're the only one who does.

POWERFUL QUESTION:

What part of your life isn't fitting you anymore?

What habits or patterns do you have that are
keeping you from having the life you want?

"It's like building a house.
You start by creating a blueprint;
only then do you begin building.
You don't just decide to build a house,
run to Home Depot,
buy whatever materials are on hand or
are on sale and start building.
Unfortunately, that's how most people
build their lives."

— TI CAINE

Building the Life of Your Dreams

I never thought I would, but I loved designing our new home with my husband. I loved having to ask myself questions like, "What kind of house do we want to live in? How much do we want to invest, and in what? How much space do we need for what purposes?" and on and on. By asking and answering these introspective, yet practical questions, we were able to confidently make all of the important big and small choices before us. The same is true for building a life. You need to know what you want.

You certainly wouldn't start a house without plans, but a lot of us plan more carefully for our vacations than we do for our lives. Before making important decisions and investments of our time, energy, and spirit, wouldn't we be well advised to stop and take time to ask ourselves some important questions?

What do you want your life to look like? A beautiful new home always starts out as a vision. My vision appeared in that framed print of a house by the sea. What's your vision? Can you see it in your mind's eye? Imagine it in all of its detail, in all of the seasons, in all of the rooms. Think in terms of "Am I going to like this? Am I going to be happy living here?" Let yourself ponder and plan.

When building the life of your dreams, you want a blueprint based on your deepest knowing about yourself - your foundation. What's your foundation? I love the imagery of this question: Do you build on rock or on sand? Think about it. What are the fundamental values and desires of your life? A good foundation is one built on self-knowledge and self-acceptance. (Don't overlook the importance of the self-acceptance piece.)

In designing your most possible life, you have dreams, desires, a blueprint and a plan. And just as you do with a house, you build from the foundation up.

"It's the possibility of having a dream come true that makes life interesting."

– PAULO COELHO FROM THE ALCHEMIST

POWERFUL QUESTION:

Do you have a dream or a vision for your life? What is it?

"She's a Seeker
Of her own Truths
Of her own Gifts
Of who she is and whose she is.
She may never know.
But it is her life's work anyway."

– SALLY HARE

Welcome to My House

I once heard a story about an old African tribal custom in which, prior to their births, children are each given a special, individual song, just for them that will carry them throughout their lives. This song is sung at all birthdays, rites of passage, and celebrations. If a child ventures into trouble, instead of being punished or chastised, she is called into a circle and her song is sung to her, to remind her of who she really is.

I have always known my song. I was born to be a teacher. This is my calling. I have loved teaching since I was a small child. I would play all day on our front porch, with the big picture window as my chalkboard. I would teach for hours to my adoring, sponge-like students. And, as my mother recalls, I always "play taught" with passion.

Then, in the third grade, I met Ms. Heidt, and I loved Ms. Heidt. Ms. Heidt was snazzy. She wore spike heels to class with her Donna Reed-style dresses. She was just plain cool…even in the decidedly uncool early 60's. Her flair alone allured me. But the one incident that tells it all about who Ms. Heidt was, and how she helped me to refine my mission, is best illustrated in this story.

My class had been assigned to give oral book reports. I don't remember why, but I hadn't read my book. Not knowing what else to do, when called upon I got up and simply made it up as I went along. It was quickly obvious to everyone — Ms. Heidt, my fellow students, and myself — that I was faking it, and badly. Ms. Heidt just let me finish. Then she smiled at me and went on with the other students. Later on, when others weren't looking, she put her arm around my shoulder and said, "Kathy, would you like to have an opportunity to try that again? I know you can do it. I believe in you."

Now, suddenly, Ms. Heidt was more than just a teacher; she was an empowerment goddess. She believed in me, she believed in my potential, and she helped me believe in me. She was wise. She understood that her goal was not to punish or humiliate me. Her goal was to show me, to teach me, and to give me the opportunity to grow.

Since that day, I have been hooked on giving other people this same experience of feeling heard, cared about, and encouraged. While my journey has been from high school teacher, to school psychologist, to graduate instructor, to psychotherapist, to life coach, all along the way I realize that what I was seeking was to be just like Ms. Heidt.

We each have a song, and that song can either be sung in our lives or not. Each of us has their own piece of music. Our particular unique gifts, if we choose to use them, will lead us to the experience that we are all in search of; fulfillment. I do not come to you as a spiritual expert. I come to you as a personal life coach. My expertise is helping you to find your song and sing it.

Over the years, I have learned a lot about motivation, visualization, and manifestation—the art of bringing your dreams into reality. I have learned about the power of silence, the power of gratitude, the power of intentions, and the power of questions. I've learned about many tools and practices that are vital to success, when we are building a life from the ground up.

I learned that we need structure, guidance, and a plan. So, in the process of stopping and sorting out my own life, I developed a life design model that helped me, and has helped others. In the process, I have learned how to be an empowerment goddess!

I encourage you to stop and take the time to ask and maybe even answer some of the powerful questions of life, so that one day you wake up and look around, and realize that you're home. And as an empowerment goddess, my job is to lovingly and gently push you the way your heart wants you to go; toward your best possible life.

POWERFUL QUESTION:

My song is to teach. What is your song?

"Most of us die with our music still inside of us..."

– OLIVER WENDELL HOLMES

"Come to the edge."
"We can't. We're afraid."
"Come to the edge."
"We can't. We will fall."
"Come to the edge."
And they came.
And she pushed them.
And they flew.

— **Appollinaire**

Creating the Design

S o why did I create this life design process? For the same reason a drowning person grabs for a rope; for my own survival. This work came out of a deep need in my own life, at a time when my success was literally killing me. *I teach what I need to learn.*

On the surface, everything looked good. I had a booming private practice seeing entirely too many clients. I was a graduate professor, and traveling up and down the East Coast as a motivational speaker. I even bought a building and became a landlord, renting office space to other mental health professionals and wellness people. I was single-parenting my daughter, doing work I loved and that I could see was valuable, and I was making good money doing it.

But underneath, things weren't so good. I call it the velvet handcuffs. I was trapped in my "success." I was a workaholic who missed her child's PTO meetings. I was overweight. I was financially insecure, not because I wasn't making a lot of money, but because I couldn't keep my books straight, so I never knew if I was spending it faster than I made it. My heart's desire was to be in a relationship, but my social life was nonexistent. If I was lucky, I'd make it to happy hour with a friend on Friday, but most of the time I couldn't even manage that. I was taking care of everybody but me, taking care of this massive house of cards I'd built. It couldn't continue. I couldn't continue.

Then, the universe came along and gave me an opportunity to stop. For a lot of us, when we get that little tap on the shoulder, it's an illness or a devastation of some type that stops us. But I got lucky. I met the man of my dreams and he wanted me to marry him.

There was a catch; because of his work, I'd have to close my successful practice and move, give up everything I'd labored so long and hard for. It took me a year, mind you, to close that practice, but I closed it. Yet all the time I was wrapping it up, I worried—now what?

I left and moved with this man out onto an island at the end of a dirt road, surrounded on three sides by a river. There were only five other houses on the island, and I didn't know a soul. My daughter, at that point, was away in school. And here I was, coming off of that workaholic lifestyle, sitting out on this island with nothing to do. For the first time in my life, I didn't have to get dressed, so I didn't.

I walked around in my pajamas most of the day, just going in circles, not knowing what to do. I think a lot of people deal with this—not really knowing what to do next, now knowing what they really want. I'd been too busy to think about it. Now, alone on the island with plenty of quiet time to reflect, I could stop and take the time to really look at my life; where I'd been, where I was, and where I was going.

And that turned out to be a whole lot tougher than I'd imagined. I was stunned. I was confused. I was lost. After years of helping other people solve problems and move forward in their lives, I didn't know what to do. I knew I didn't want to just blindly chase after the next whim, that I wanted to stop and get centered within myself again. I wanted to make the higher choices for my life. And if not now, when?

Out of this authentic experience, in the moment of my own personal need, I sat down and designed a powerfully philosophical yet pragmatic program for personal growth and transformation. Always having been a teacher and a student, I asked in my teacher voice: When a person is in the act of making decisions about where to go, considering their possible next step, what do they need? What did I need?

Everything came to me in questions—all kinds of questions, the questions I would ask someone if they had come to me and asked for my help.

*Good questions open the doors to all
of the possibilities....*

– KENNETH FOSTER

POWERFUL QUESTION:

What is the first question you would want me
to ask you, if you came to me for help?

This work isn't about changing,
it's about growing into your life.

– KATHY MURPHY

An Organic Life

I n my life on the island, by the water, I had to admit to myself that I actually hadn't been doing the kind of work that I wanted to be doing with people. Not really. I'd been trained to help people to change — but on some level I had to admit that I'd always been uncomfortable with that word "change." For me, the idea of change implied an underlying accusation that there was something wrong with us to begin with.

Finally, it came to me. The real work that I wanted to be doing with people was growth. That may sound like word games, but it's much more than that. When someone is asking us to change, our natural human instinct is to resist it. But very few people resist the pull to grow. People want to grow. That's a natural thing to be pulled toward, and much easier work when we get in touch with who we really are, and then start moving in that direction. That subtle shift for me, switching gears from the word "change" to "growth" and "transformation," just popped me alive.

Growth and transformation are good and natural processes. This is not about being pathologically driven to achieve yet another to-do list. This is about our innate, human drive to grow. Renowned humanist psychologist, Carl Rogers says that just as the acorn is programmed to grow into a majestic oak tree, and a sea turtle is programmed to seek the vast ocean, we too are driven to become who we are meant to be.

Trust me, who you are meant to be is good. Your unique, individual potential is implanted in you, just as in the seeds of a tree or a flower. Whether you are a giant live oak tree or a beautiful, flowering magnolia tree, or a dainty orchid— all this may vary. But you have a potential. And it is your own personal, beautiful potential. It is your birthright. Given proper sunlight and watering, the trees and flowers grow into their potential. And so do we.

For those of you who say that you don't have a clue as to your gifts or your possibilities, don't worry, you really do. You get glimpses of it all the time. It shows up in who and what you admire in your life. It shows up in your interests, in your desires and, of course, in your dreams. It shows up in your longings. It shows up in what gets your attention. And if you pay attention, you can find yours.

You do have an inner guidance system, an inner voice that will wake you up and guide you to grow into your most possible life. Whether you call it soul, intuition, self-awareness or intelligence, it will inform you and help you. It is the voice that will guide you home - once you've learned to ask, and then to listen.

"Even if you live to be 100,
it's really a very short time.
So why not spend it undergoing
this process of evolution,
of opening your mind and heart,
connecting with your true nature...
rather than getting better and better at
fixing, grasping, and closing doors."
— PEMA CHODRON, *Noble Heart*

POWERFUL QUESTION:

What do you feel you are being called to grow in your life?

"A time comes in your life when you finally get it...
When in the midst of all your fears and your tears
You stop dead in your tracks
And somewhere the voice inside you head cries out -
ENOUGH....

Slowly you begin to take responsibility for yourself....

With courage in your heart,
You take a stand
You take a deep breath
And you begin to live the life you know
You were meant to be living."

– AUTHOR UNKNOWN

"Tell me, what is it that you plan to do with your one wild and precious life?"

– MARY OLIVER

A Well-
Built Life

T aking the time to stop and figure out who we really are and what we really want is the work of life design. It requires a lot of attention. It requires honesty, courage, commitment, and more. People ask me all the time, why bother? What's the benefit of going through all the work and effort to figure this out?

When our outer lives (what we do), match our inner lives (our values and our gifts), we are in alignment. This is when our head, heart, and gut are lined up, in agreement, and focused. We are in the flow. Athletes call it being in the zone. You've heard about it. You've experienced it. It's a proven psychological phenomenon. When we get to that place where everything just flows smoother, life is more exciting, we feel more fulfilled, we feel more vitality, we feel "on purpose." We all have examples of this in our lives.

Take a second and remember the last time you felt really in the zone, where time slipped by, when you felt like you were shining, or on fire, or however you define that ultimate feeling.

What were you doing?

Take a moment and really remember it.

Remember how you felt. Really freeze-frame the feeling.

This is what you're looking for. This is what we are all truly seeking; these feelings of being vital, alive, energized, on purpose. This is how you want to be living your life. You want to be living life as if it is an adventure. You want to feel mentally sharp and alert. You want to be overwhelmed with gratitude and comfortable with yourself. You want to be pleased with your life.

Does this describe how you feel? If not, help is here. Knowing who you are and what you want, and committing to taking the next steps in your life, will take you home; back to feeling vital, alive, energized and on purpose. This is what we are all seeking.

Remember the metaphysical law of the universe,
what you are seeking, seeks you.

POWERFUL QUESTION:

What feelings are you looking for in your life? Satisfaction, excitement, peace? What is it that you are seeking?

Waiting for Serendipity

What Do You Do When You Don't Know?

Note of caution: There will be times in our lives when the dreams aren't there, the visions don't come, and the faith is weak. Sometimes you're more receptive, more able, and more open and ready. Some days, it's just simply too much—not today. Some days the best you can do is just put one foot in front of the other; left foot, right foot, breathe, breathe, breathe. Some days that's all we can manage, and that's okay.

What then? Given that I'm a life coach who specializes in helping people to "move their lives forward," people are often surprised when my advice is to slow down and do nothing. If this is you and you don't know what to do, one option is to do nothing at all.

This makes a lot of sense, but it isn't easy. We like knowing. We like doing. We are addicted to making things happen and moving things forward. I'm all for that. But what do you do when you genuinely don't know what direction to go in? When you don't remember what your heart desires? What do you do when you've lost your vision for your life? My advice is to do nothing.

When I say do nothing, it's really a paradoxical suggestion, because when you stop doing, even for only a short while, you are doing the most important personal work of all. When we stop doing and moving so much, we may be able to hear the small, inner voice. Your wisdom and guidance, your most possible life, comes from deep inside and from listening with your heart, not from over-thinking and certainly not from overdoing. Sometimes we just need to get still, listen, and maybe wait for serendipity or grace, or a synchronicity or two.

Serendipity, grace, synchronicities—all of these are beautiful words to describe when the magic happens. You know those times—when suddenly things come together—the "aha!" moments, the insights, the energy, the gifts of life. They turn up when we're simply taking a walk or doing a mundane chore like cleaning the floor.

Synchronicities are those unexplained and fortunate coincidences, like when the very book you need for an article you are writing just mysteriously appears. Or when someone you meet in line at a party turns out to be exactly the person you need to meet in your profession. At these moments, something magical and mysterious happens, and our lives start to move with the flow again. This is what serendipity feels like, when everything fits and flows.

When there is no flow in your life, at the very least, stop swimming upstream. Slow down. Sometimes you just need to rest. I believe that most of us are really tired. We are physically, emotionally, and spiritually exhausted. We need deep, replenishing rest. Yet we don't give it to ourselves.

Last year I found myself getting way too busy with so many (all good) things that revved up my life to a breakneck pace. This happens to all of us. We take on additional projects on top of our already-overbooked lives and, before we know it, we're off and running. My husband and I built and moved into a new home that I love. I wrote the major portion of the manuscript for this book. I did retreats and workshops all over the place, and put a lot of hours into our Retreats by Design business. I was coaching clients, running women's groups, and writing programs. I also had a huge love affair going on with my husband.

While I adored all of this, I found that my energy and creativity had packed up and moved on. I had gotten so caught up in the day-to-day chores and things-to-do that I'd lost focus on the vision - the real things I wanted for my life, the important stuff like peace and serenity. And I was bone-tired. So I took a vacation and, while that certainly helped, at the end of it I was still weary, and still couldn't see the vision for my life.

When you've lost your vision, what do you do? Slow down and wait. Begin this inner work of just being. Begin by asking yourself powerful questions. Then get still and listen. Listen for the wisdom of your life.

I looked around my life and took inventory of what I could shelve for a while, what I could say "no" to, and what I really needed. First of all, I needed some careless time; time to just be, time with nothing to do, and no nagging to-do list. You have to be the one to give yourself this, because no one else will. In American culture, we are expected to be busy all the time. When I told a close friend what I was doing –"Nothing, as little as possible"– she said, "And you don't feel guilty?"

I explained to her that I really wasn't doing "nothing," but that I was resting, preparing, and waiting; waiting for serendipity, waiting for grace, waiting for guidance. I also told her that I was healing from a period of overdoing. I told her that I was taking time to do some of the solitary, quiet work of personal growth. I started working less (the chores can wait), watching less TV, reading more, journaling daily, meditating, walking, and being very, very silent. There was no radio in the car or distracting noise in the house—except for the birds chirping.

There was more communing with myself, God, and the Universe (and some loved ones). My daily affirmation was "I am open and receptive to the power of grace and wisdom in my life." I made a vow not to make any major decisions until I felt the impulse to move coming from deep within. I made a commitment to not do anything until I really knew what it was that I wanted, and I promised myself that I would have the courage to move forward with the information I received. Now, this is what life by design is all about!

Also, a good life design process isn't something that you do one time and that's it. We need something we can use over and over, day by day, minute by minute. Think of this book as a Do-It-Yourself manual, a workbook for when you are ready to slow down and do the work of rediscovering, re-grounding, and rededicating your life, complete with all the tools you'll need for the process.

If this isn't resonating for you today, put it down. Pick it up another time. But when you're ready, there's a process for you here; there's help. It's help you can return to again and again, a process you can repeat when you need it. One of the reasons I'm writing this book now is because I needed it again. I needed to be reminded, and I needed to do the work myself. So, join me on the journey.

POWERFUL QUESTION:

Are you ready? Are you ready to go on a journey back to yourself?

PART III

Your Possible Life Design

"*To be what we are,*

and to become what we are capable of becoming,

is the only end of life."

— ROBERT LOUIS STEVENSON

I I I

A woman I worked with named Sandy had recently been through major transitions and losses in her life; divorce, aging mother, aging self, business sold, only child now married. One day she realized that her old life was gone. After much grieving and quite a bit of fear, she knew she had a decision to make. She could grow…or not. The inner voice that loved her was waking her up in the middle of the night saying, "Now, now is the time."

The work of growth and transformation begins when you let yourself hear the call. "Wake up," Oriah Mountain Dreamer says. "Do not stay asleep. Remember who you are and let this knowing take you home." When you find yourself holding your head, asking "Now what?" this is your beginning. You have begun to ask the powerful questions. The journey has begun.

And you're never too young or too old to get started! I've got clients in their eighties. I got an email from one just the other day. She's 82 years old, and (I swear it's true) at 82 she decided to move out of the little condo she'd been living in forever, and move to Charlotte to be near friends she loves and to be where exciting things are going on. And of course she's terrified and people think she's nuts. Her email's full of "I'm scared as hell, but I had to do it." The great Jewish thinker, Rabbi Hillel said, "If not now, when?" My 82-year-old friend asked herself the same powerful question—and decided there was no better time than now.

Welcome to Your Possible Life Design Process, the work of stopping and taking some time to build the life of your dreams. It begins with groundwork. In the beginning, you want to be aware of how the overall building process works and the tools that you will need. We'll start with the popular Wheel of Life coaching exercise to take a quick preliminary look at where you are and where you want to grow.

After you have learned some of the tools for personal growth work, next comes excavating for the foundation. Through several exercises, you will be led to answer the first of the most powerful questions of all: Who Am I? Really? The "Really" question initiates the process of digging deeper.

You will also be designing a blueprint, a vision for your life. The powerful design questions here are:

- *"What do I Really Want?"*

- *"What is my Life Purpose?"*

- *"What's my Vision?" and…*

- *"What's my Personal Philosophy?"*

When what you do is directly related to who you are and what you think is important, you will feel satisfied, fulfilled, and full of life. This is living in alignment. This work will help you so much with the choices you make daily. You will learn to make these choices from a deep, loving place of self-knowledge and self-love. For the planning stages of your life design, the powerful questions are:

- *"What are my Obstacles?"*

- *"What do I Need?" and…*

- *"What am I Willing to Do Next?"*

At the end of this process you will have a plan, your plan, in the form of a list of next steps, an empowered list of possibilities; each one has grown out of your deepest self-knowing. Your possibilities become your next steps.

Going through the entire process, my client, Sandy, determined that her three greatest longings were to be happy and peaceful, to enjoy her life more, and to feel better about herself. She began the process of dreaming, visualizing, and drawing a plan. She asked herself what kind of lifestyle she aspired to. What would it look like? What character traits were most important to her? Who did she really think she was, and what was it that she really wanted? What did she wish to express in her life now? She allowed herself to see a bigger vision for her life, a true home designed by her heart's deepest longings.

She drew out a comprehensive plan for all the rooms of her house. She began to figure out how to bring happiness into her life. She set a physical goal for exercise. She set a spiritual goal for regular meditation and journaling. She also signed up for a yoga class.

She learned to use tools like meditating and journaling, as well as the major power tools of commitment, discipline and accountability. She made a plan to use music and inspirational readings regularly, as well as knowing when to retreat into stillness. She learned the power of setting intentions and asking herself the powerful questions in her life. She developed a personal philosophy to keep her focused and energized. She began to build her life, step by step.

Every good house design always prepares for the possibility of needing to add on at some point in the future. Because, as everyone knows, you're never, ever finished; a life, as well as a house is always an ongoing process. Sandy, however, now had the tools and the process that she could use throughout her life for its inevitable future expansion. When all was said and done, she had a life design built on values, positive beliefs, passion and purpose, ready for even further growth.

POWERFUL QUESTION:

When do you think would be a good time to start
living your true life? Is this a possibility?

"A good life…is built brick by brick."

– JOHAN CHRISTOPH ARNOLD

The Groundwork

Thus begins the first step for building your new home, the sacred and special place in which you want to live. I love using the metaphor of building a house, and/or building a life. Both call forth our creativity and our dreaming, as well as require a lot of work, (And I hate to tell you, but it is work. It's work that flows more easily the more you do it, but it's still work.) Doing the groundwork is looking at where you are now, looking ahead to where you want to go, and assembling the tools necessary for the job.

Early on, it's helpful to do a quick assessment of where we are and the areas in which we might want to grow. The Wheel of Life is a fun and visually powerful source of information about how satisfied/dissatisfied we are, that helps us see where we need to focus our work.

How satisfied are you in your current life? Carl Rogers says that one of the most reliable predictors of emotional health is the gap between where you think you are and where you want to be - the bigger the gap, the greater your unrest and dissatisfaction. How wide is the gap between where you currently are, and where you want to be? How big is the gap between what you say you believe, and what you actually do? (Don't worry if the gap is huge, because you will actually learn how to use it to help you move forward.)

The Wheel of Life exercise is when you take your first comprehensive look at the major areas of your life, and it is also your introduction to a picture of what your full and balanced life will look like. The Wheel represents the total experience of our lives. For the sake of guidance, names are given for seven of the eight areas. One is left blank for you to decide the topic; in fact, if you want, you can choose all the topics. This is about you.

This is the first Design Sheet of the process. You'd be wise to make extra copies of this, because it's an assessment tool which you will want to use frequently. My husband and I do them every year. We each do an assessment of individual satisfaction, and we do one as a couple. This stimulates a lot of discussion between us about our aspirations and dreams. It's a very helpful tool for starting meaningful conversations.

Take a few minutes to do your Wheel of Life.
(Design Sheet #1—page 70)

The Wheel provides a stunning visual about where you may be feeling out of balance, and is a great starting point to begin taking a look at your life. At first glance, does your wheel look the way you want it to? Is your "ride" smooth or bumpy? One woman told me her ride wasn't bumpy at all, it was flat.

Can you see areas in which you'd like to grow? As you reflect on the wheel, you will actually begin to see where the gaps, the needs and your desires are. This information will help you know where you want to get started, what tools you may need, and the rooms you want to build.

After you've completed the first assessment on the Wheel of Life, go back and ask yourself, "In each area of my life, where would I like to be in one year?" For example, if you rated yourself currently a 3 in your spiritual life, that's okay, but where would you like to be next year? An 8 or a 9, or maybe even a 10? Go thoughtfully over each area and rate where you'd like to be a year from today.

Now ask yourself, what would it take to get there from here? What would it take to move my level of satisfaction with my spiritual life from a 3 to an 8 in the next year? Again, just let yourself imagine. As ideas come to you, write them down. Your list might say things like pray every day, read more enlightened books, go to church, be more forgiving, and meditate daily or study spirituality. You get the picture. Now, that's powerful. But, don't worry so much now about the next steps, we'll work on those later. For now, just begin the process of acknowledging where you are, and maybe catch a glimpse of where you want to grow.

Design Sheet #1:
How Smooth is Your Ride?

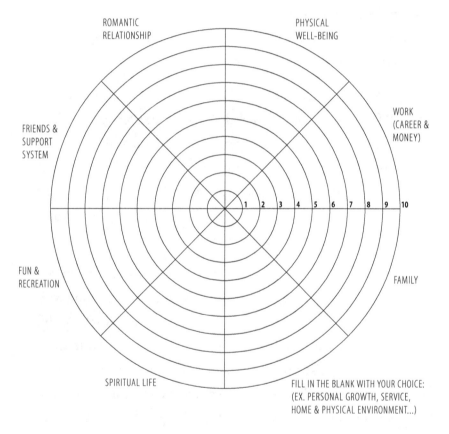

ROMANTIC RELATIONSHIP

PHYSICAL WELL-BEING

WORK (CAREER & MONEY)

FRIENDS & SUPPORT SYSTEM

1 2 3 4 5 6 7 8 9 10

FUN & RECREATION

FAMILY

SPIRITUAL LIFE

FILL IN THE BLANK WITH YOUR CHOICE: (EX. PERSONAL GROWTH, SERVICE, HOME & PHYSICAL ENVIRONMENT...)

In each of the areas on the circle the center of the wheel is 0 and the outer edge is 10, the most satisfying. Rate each area in terms of your level of satisfaction and then color in the individual section. Then take a look. The new perimeter of the circle represents the "Wheel of Your Life." How smooth is your ride?

POWERFUL QUESTIONS:

What are the two lowest satisfaction scores?

How much time per day do you spend in these areas?

What are your two highest scores?

How much time per day do you spend in these?

"Whatever good things we build...
end up building us."

– JIM ROHN

Tools for Life Design

From the Wheel of Life, you begin to see a blueprint appearing in front of you. You are already getting glimpses and ideas about what's missing and where you want to build. You are ready to begin the work. This will require tools.

Learning about these tools is very important. Gloria Steinem says the real payoff for doing life design work is not about the goals, the outcomes or the issues. Rather, it's about the process and the practices. These organic practices, these tools for life design, are in and of themselves the true desired results. These are the things that we want to take away and use daily - things like journaling and inspirational music and reading.

In the following pages, many tools are presented. Some are standard, well-tested, well-loved practices; others are unique to this program. These are all the tools and practices I've come to rely on over the many years of both being a seeker and a teacher. They can be used for every step of the life design process, and for every step of your life.

List of Tools Necessary for Building the Life of Your Dreams

THE ESSENTIAL TOOLS:

1. Being a Possibility Thinker
2. Asking the Powerful Questions of Your Life

TOOLS FOR CREATING A SAFE SPACE IN WHICH TO ASK THE POWERFUL QUESTIONS:

1. Heart Centeredness
2. Retreating
3. Sharing
4. The Willingness to Be Real
5. Intentions
6. Meditation
7. Journaling
8. Inspirational Reading and Music
9. Gratitude

THE POWER TOOLS
(AFTER GOING THROUGH THE LIFE DESIGN PROCESS, YOU'LL BE READY TO WORK WITH THESE):

1. Knowing Your Truth
2. Commitment and Discipline
3. Accountability and Support

The Essential Tools

Essential Tool #1:
Being a Possibility Thinker

*Believing in the possibilities of your life
is the power of this program.*

Believing in possibility is the piece that makes this process different from all of the many other goal-setting and life design models out there. What do you believe are the possibilities for your life?

You must be willing to clap to save Tinker Bell. You must believe that you have the personal power to co-create your life, and that you are not a helpless pawn, subject to the unfathomable whims of the universe.

Just recently, my husband and I took a big leap of faith. Following my deep passion to teach and to help others, we moved again. This time, my husband quit his job to follow me. It is the ultimate story of believing in possibilities, for him to leave his paying job in support of my dream. When we were making our decision, we used the mantra "Leap and the net will appear." Since we are still in the process of manifesting this dream, every once in a while he'll ask me if I've seen the net! This business of living your one true life requires a lot of faith.

A man found an eagle's egg and put it in a nest of a barnyard hen. The eaglet hatched with the brood of chicks and grew up with them. All of her life the eagle did what the barnyard chicks did, thinking she was a barnyard chicken, too. She scratched the earth for worms and insects. She clucked and cackled, and she would thrash her wings around, and sometimes even fly a few feet in the air.

Years passed and the eagle grew older. One day she saw a magnificent bird above in the cloudless sky. It glided in graceful majesty upon the powerful wind on golden wings. "That's an eagle," said a neighbor. "She belongs in the sky. We're chickens. We belong to the earth." So the eagle lived and died a chicken, for that's what she thought she was.

— *Anthony de Mello, Founder of Miraval*

While I love telling this story of the eagle who grew up believing she was a chicken, my daughter hates it. She says it's too sad. The poor sweet bird never knew she had the potential or the possibility. But you're not about to follow the eagle's example. You know, deep down inside, that your life can be so much more fulfilling and satisfying. And you intuitively know you are capable of soaring, too. I promise you, you are capable of so much more than you realize.

Do you believe? and *Is it a possibility?* are questions that will be used continually and strategically throughout this entire process, and are what makes it unique. For example: In the *Visualizing Your Life Exercise,* after every vision you write down, you will be guided to search within for information as to whether you believe the vision is a possibility for you or not.

If a vision does not feel true for you, you keep dreaming the vision until you have crafted one that still pushes you to grow, but that you can believe in. At each step of the life design worksheet, you will be asked to search within and answer from the heart, with courage and honesty, "Is this a possibility?"

You may be asking "Am I supposed to be dreaming big, or just within the limits of my possibilities?" I say "Dream big!" Trust me, your true potentials and possibilities are huge. You can dream big and, at the same time, create a dream that you can believe in. There is enough room between where you are now and where you want to be that you can come up with big, big dreams, visions, and goals. But you will also learn to dream the next step. Next steps will get you to the ultimate big dream. You will be building your most possible life.

"Start by doing what is necessary,
then do what's possible,
and suddenly you are doing the impossible."
— ST. FRANCIS OF ASSISI

There are so many inspirational stories about what people have accomplished and I am sure you have some from your own experiences, stories of things you've achieved that initially seemed beyond your limits. Take a moment to remember a time when you did something that you'd not thought at the beginning you could do. Some of mine were quitting smoking, natural childbirth, and earning a Ph.D. What are your personal stories of seemingly impossible goals that you've reached? How'd you do it?

_____

_____

_____

_____

_____

_____

_____

_____

_____

_____

_____

_____

POWERFUL QUESTION:

Name one desire that today feels like an impossibility for your life.

Could this be a possibility? Think about it.

If you believed you were smart,
you'd act smart.
If you believed you were creative,
you'd act creative.
If you believed you were a success,
you'd act successful.
If you believed you were excellent at something,
you'd act excellent.

It can't be said enough times. What you believe will, for the most part, be what you get. And if you don't believe? Well, you know what happens. Stop for a moment and honestly ask yourself; what do you believe? It is the most fundamental power source that we have; the power of our thoughts. What kinds of thoughts dominate your inner life? It is important to be aware of them, because your thoughts are what dominate and create your outer life.

What are your basic beliefs and attitudes about yourself, others, and the world? Do you believe that life is abundant and purposeful, or empty? Do you believe that you are strong, competent, capable and lovable...or not? Do you believe that you have the personal power to live the life of your dreams...or that no such thing exists? What is your philosophy for living?

What do you say to yourself and to others? Have you ever stopped to listen to yourself? Have you ever stopped to consider what your philosophy about life is? What you choose to believe, in my opinion, is the most critical piece of the life design process. And, interestingly, it is one thing over which we have complete control.

I am what I think I am.
You are what I think you are.
The world is what I think it is.
Ah, the power!

Let's take a few minutes and focus on what makes our thoughts so powerful. Thoughts you have repeated over and over to yourself become your automatic and even unconscious beliefs. Thoughts are energy, and they fuel your feelings and your actions. Seriously, they literally contain physical energy that has an identifiable physiological and psychological effect on you. Your thoughts can either energize or de-energize you.

I love to teach people what I call the T-F-B cycle. It is both powerful and magical to understand this dynamic interplay: Your Thoughts—*T* - (what you say to yourself when you perceive something) create Feelings—*F* - (how you feel about what happened to you) which then leads to Behavior—*B* (what you do in response to what happened to you).

Not only will you believe what you tell yourself and act accordingly (the self-fulfilling prophecy), you will continue to repeat this process. The cycle gets repeated over and over, which reinforces the original Thought, and on, and on, and on, until it becomes a Belief.

You can bring about transformation in your life by changing any one of these three areas of the cycle– your thoughts, your feelings, or your behavior. Psychologists originally believed that if you could simply change your behavior (just stop doing what you're doing, or start doing something different) then feelings and thoughts would subsequently change. And this does happen—but it's often difficult to "Just Say No." Then, we believed that if we could change our feelings, this would be the key to breaking the cycle. So, we medicated and "therapized" our feelings, and we felt better -- but it was still exceedingly hard to change our behavior.

The power for true, lasting transformation, I believe, is in changing our thoughts. Most of the time this is the origin, the beginning point of the cycle and the most effective place to break it. The self-fulfilling prophecy has been proven to be true too many times to count. It is what you believe to be true that will most likely come true. We all know this.

We all have beliefs about the world. *The task is to be conscious of our beliefs, and to be aware of the energy that our beliefs carry.* Wake up and pay attention to what you think and say. You know that if your beliefs and self-talk are negative, you won't get what you want. You know if your beliefs are uplifting and empowering, you are much more likely to rise to meet them and achieve your goals. Know which thoughts and beliefs energize you, and which ones take your energy away.

There are so many powerful questions to be asked in order to explore your philosophy about life. Things like: Do you believe in personal responsibility? Do you believe in community? Do you believe that "*#@! happens"? What do you really believe about yourself? Do you believe that you are powerful? Tell the truth! Now is the opportunity to review some of your attitudes, thoughts and beliefs. Think about which ones help you, and which ones hurt you. Rewrite those that are not working for you. You will learn to work with this skill specifically in Step 2 of the Life Design Worksheet.

Develop a personal philosophy about you and your life that works for you. Take a moment to reflect on Design Sheet #2 (page 84)—*What is Your Personal Philosophy?*

POWERFUL QUESTION:

Do you believe that you can transform your
world by changing how you think?

Design Sheet #2:
WHAT IS YOUR PERSONAL PHILOSOPHY?

When prompted by the list of subjects on the opposite page, pay attention to the first thoughts/stereotypes that come to mind. Write them out. Answer quickly and spontaneously. Tell the truth. Then allow yourself to look with softer eyes at the effect these beliefs have on how you live your life. How did you come to formulate these opinions? Do they work? Do they uplift your life? Do they energize, or de-energize? Are they negative, or positive?

For example, when I ask myself, "What do I really believe about powerful women," I write that I believe powerful women can change the world and that we have a responsibility and an obligation to be active and engaged. I believe that powerful women are leaders. I believe that women are becoming more and more powerful every day. I also believe that women still have to overcome unfair biases and stereotypes. I believe there are a lot of payoffs to being a powerful woman, but I also believe there are costs associated with being a powerful woman.

I conclude that generally I have a very positive belief system around powerful women, yet am still aware that women generally have paid a price in our world.

What I believe about:

Powerful Women

Rich People

Poor People

Overweight People

Thin People

Politicians

Men

Myself

My Own Personal Power

You get the idea; add your own groups/topics!

Go back through each of these beliefs and ask if they energize or de-energize your life. Could you develop a new set of beliefs?

"Our deepest fear is not that we are inadequate.
Our deepest fear is that we are powerful beyond measure."

– NELSON MANDELA

Jana Stanfield has an unbelievably inspiring song entitled *What Would I Do Today If I Were Brave?* I use it in all of my retreats, workshops and presentations. I also use it for my own personal journaling. The song says *"if I were brave I'd walk the razor's edge where fools and angels dare to tread."* Ask yourself -- what would you do or be in your life if you were brave?

I'd be a possibility thinker. About everything. Always. This would be my credo for living. This requires being brave. It takes courage to dare to dream and to create again. It requires the heart of an adventurer. Possibility thinking requires a willingness to think what you've never thought. Possibility thinkers aren't concerned about what they are, but with what they can be. Possibility thinking goes beyond positive thinking into a world of abundance, a world of all that can be. Possibility thinking requires that one be a seeker. If I were brave, I'd always be a possibility thinker about everything and everybody, every day. I encourage you to come and walk the razor's edge with me.

POWERFUL QUESTION:

What philosophy do you live by?

So, are you a possibility thinker?

Come and take a journey with me now. Just for a moment, let yourself imagine. For now, no writing, just dreaming. For just a moment - *Consider the Possibilities…*

> *There is a meditation script in the back of this book (page 216) and also a 10-minute audio recording of this meditation on my website (www.kathymurphyphd.com). This is a provocative journey into our dreams. Use Jana Stanfield's **If I Were Brave** music. You can download it on iTunes or go to her website.*

On the next page is a short version of a list of questions meant to start the process of opening you to dream again about your possibilities. As you contemplate these questions, see yourself with soft eyes. Drop the harshness, the judgment, and the negative commentary, and just let yourself…

Consider the possibility that you could
have the life of your dreams…

What would that look like? The life of your dreams…

What would you see for your emotional life?

Imagine yourself living an emotionally expressive, wonderful life.

What would you see for your love life?

Imagine your ideal loving relationship(s). See it as a possibility.

What does your dream physical and health state look like?
Is it a possibility?

What would you be willing to do differently here?

Describe your most creative self.

What would you like to achieve intellectually?

How do you see yourself career-wise and financially?

What commitments would you like to make in these areas?

Describe your inner and outer spiritual life.
What could you do to move it into better alignment?

Are these ideas possibilities? Is this life possible for you?

"I worked for a menial's hire,
Only to learn dismayed,
That any wage I had asked of life,
Life would have willingly paid."

—Anonymous poet

Essential Tool #2:
Asking the Powerful
Questions of Your Life

"Whenever you ask yourself a question, You are
fine-tuning your mind to seek the answer."

– KENNETH D. FOSTER

I think I would have loved Socrates. I love the power of good questions. I love both the asking and the answering, although the asking is easier. My husband rolls his eyes at my never-ending questions. But I love the power of questions. Good questions push us. Good questions open the door to possibilities. They cause us to have to stop and think, to assess, to contemplate, and to decide. After over twenty-five years working as a psychotherapist, I know the value of good questions. A well-asked, well-timed question can open us right up and help us find answers we didn't even know we had.

Remember the proverb, "Ask and ye shall receive"? One of my deep beliefs is that if you don't ask for something, you probably won't get it. I've always been open to asking for help. However, this is about asking your deep, inner wisdom to help you. The questions of life design are about asking your soul to speak up and offer wisdom and guidance. If you learn to ask, you just may hear the voice that knows your name, calling you back home to yourself.

In this life design process you will be given opportunities to reflect on many questions about who you are, what you want, how you feel about certain things. You will be asked questions at the end of each section. Most of the Design Sheets are structured processes for asking powerful questions.

A lot of us feel that we simply *can't* answer these types of questions. I've heard and seen all kinds of reactions from blank and empty stares to complete meltdowns. Mostly I hear, "I don't know." We need support. I know I did.

People can become overwhelmed when asked to share their heart's longings. It requires a great deal of courage to move in the direction of our inner guidance. Asking and answering the powerful questions of your life will require your willingness to be vulnerable, your willingness to share, and your willingness to speak your truth. Only you can give yourself permission to respond with truth from the heart. It can be scary but, believe me, it's worth it.

"To the question of your life,
You are the only answer."
– J. COUDER

POWERFUL QUESTIONS:

*Go through the following lists of questions (or add your own).
Every so often, choose one and take some time to consider and
record your answers. Use these wonderful questions to stimulate
reflection, journaling or conversation.*

1.   What was your childhood dream?

2.   What did you most love to do as a child?

3.   What is the main feeling that you want to experience in your life?

4.   What makes you happy?

5.   What are your talents?

6.   What are you passionate about?

7.   What are you most committed to in your life?

8.   What do you value most?

9.   What is the biggest obstacle in your life right now?

10. What do you need to say no to in your life?

11. What do you need to say yes to in your life?

12. What one thing would most make a difference in the quality
     of your life?

13. What is one thing you have in your life that you really,
     really don't need?

14. If you were just starting out in your life, what would you do
     differently?

15. What do you most want to be remembered for when you die?

16. What would you do if you absolutely knew you could not fail?

17. What would be the best use of your life?

18. What support do I need for my own growth and to achieve my goals?

"Who you are and what you want are not simple questions; most people live their entire lives without answering them."

—GARY ZUKAV

We ask ourselves many powerful questions throughout this process but it really breaks down into three basic, main questions. The three most powerful questions of all are:

1. Who Am I? Really?

2. What Do I Really Want?

3. Knowing This, How Then Shall I Live?

These 3 questions form the foundation, the blueprint, and the plan for your life. Your foundation is built from the most powerful question of all, Who Am I? The blueprint comes from envisioning What Do I Really Want? And the design for our lives comes from Knowing This, How Shall I Live? This can be difficult work. Before you go into the process of asking the most powerful questions of your life, you will definitely need some more tools—tools to help you create a safe space to go within.

There once was a priest walking on his journey when he happened upon a military sentry posted at the entrance to the road. The sentry demanded of the priest, "Who are you? What do you want? Where are you going?" The priest was taken aback. Upon deep reflection, he answered. "You know, I don't know the answers to those questions, but I tell you what, I will give you $100 to ask me those same questions every day of my life."

You are on a Journey

A Journey to Rediscover

Who You Really Are

What You Really Want

and What the Possibilities are for Your Life...

*"The soul is shy like a wild animal,
it seeks safety in the underbrush...
and must be coaxed out."*

—PARKER PALMER

Tools for Creating a Safe Space

What do I mean, by "creating a safe space"? In preparing to do this work, you just don't sit down at the dinner table with the TV blaring, or in an agitated or a tired state. You have to be thoughtful and mindful. My job, when I work with people, is to create the physical place and the emotional space to ask the powerful questions of our lives.

As you read this book and begin your own personal self-exploration, I want you to pay attention to creating the space and the place that will help you to get beneath the layers and move out of your rational logical mind and into your heart, the part of yourself that really knows, loves, and believes in you.

The following are some tools for creating a safe space for the soul to show up and offer its guidance.

CREATING A SPACE, TOOL #1:
HEART-CENTEREDNESS

"There is a wisdom of the head, and...a wisdom of the heart!"

– CHARLES DICKENS

You've heard it from others. You've heard yourself doing it. Talking strictly out of your head. You know it, that intellectual script that is usually telling us how things are, how they have always been done, and how they will continue to be done. While at times navigating our world truly requires a thinking, logical perspective, in matters of visualizing, designing and living the life of our dreams, a heart calling is probably more helpful.

There's a difference when I'm talking from my heart, as opposed to from my head. The heart has a knowledge all its own. The heart has its own voice. In all likelihood, this is where the wisdom of the soul resides. When in the process of life design work, and particularly when answering the deeper questions of your life, seek to speak from the heart.

Heart-Centeredness is the practice of dropping down, out of our intellectual self, out of our minds, and into our heart; dropping down to a different source of both information and power. This is a critical component of this process. If we ask, and if we will learn to listen, the heart will give us guidance and clues into the longings of our soul and the purpose of our lives.

So, how does one learn to drop from the head to the heart to harvest this rich information? For some people this is a natural skill that comes easily; for some of us it requires a shift, a remembering to drop down. There are many portals to the heart. You will want to practice opening the heart and dropping down to where your truth resides.

Take a moment and place your hands over your heart. Feel the energy that comes from the heart. From the study of the chakras, we find that the heart is the gateway between the lower energy centers which are involved in such issues as trust and self esteem, and the higher centers in the throat and the head which control the more spiritual dimensions of our experience. From these higher centers comes choice and higher vision. When the heart is open, we're more able to access the higher dimensions of our being-ness.

There are so many practices and entire religions that teach us how to open our hearts. This is probably the greatest spiritual practice of all. This really requires intention, mindfulness, and commitment. Throughout the process of life design, and specifically when we go through the Design Sheets, we will call upon this tool.

Your vision will become clear only when
you look into your heart.

– CARL JUNG

POWERFUL QUESTION:

Do you know the voice of your wisdom?

How does your voice speak to you?

To know yourself,

to know what you want,

to discover why you are here,

you want to get quiet with yourself.

You want to take time to go inside yourself.

You want to get still enough, quiet enough,

to hear your own life speak to you.

If you take time to center yourself every day,

take time to move towards the very

essence of who you are,

your life will begin to unfold differently.

– OPRAH'S "LIVE YOUR BEST LIFE" PROGRAM

"If we step away for a time, we are not, as many would accuse, being irresponsible, but, rather, we are preparing ourselves to more ably perform our duties and obligations."

— MAYA ANGELOU

Retreating sounds like we're running away, but it's not that. Retreating is about giving yourself the space to experience stillness - a quiet space in which you can begin to hear the whisper of your intuition, to journey back to yourself, your needs, your desires, and to tell the truth about your strengths, your weaknesses, what you want and what you don't want, and what you will and won't do.

The retreat experience is very different from a relaxation experience. While being relaxed is a crucial component to a successful retreat, it is not the end result. Rather, the end goal is a clearer vision of yourself and your life path; to reconnect with yourself, the universe, your higher power, your dreams, your purpose.

If you come to my weekend retreats, or if you come to my day retreats, everything is designed to help you step away from your busy world for the purpose of taking that inner journey back to yourself. In these experiences, we take care of your physical needs, like food and lodging. We create a warm and relaxing environment. We usually gather at a nature retreat center or at a spa, and I've created an entire program designed to facilitate a fruitful, enriching inner journey. A formal retreat is a very powerful tool for rediscovering, rejuvenating and recommitting yourself to your life.

Not all of us can go on a formal retreat, as least not as often as we'd like. And while we all agree that taking time to be relaxed, contemplative, and mindful about our lives is a worthwhile thing, we still don't do it. We're too busy. Being busy is a given for most of us. And the truth is, we're probably not going to get any less busy. Ironically, when we take time to retreat, time seems to expand, and you approach your tasks with a more peaceful heart, open mind, and relaxed attitude.

But a retreat doesn't have to be an elaborate escape. Personal mini-retreats can range from spending the weekend alone in silence and contemplation, to just taking a walk on the beach or in the woods for the purpose of reconnecting with yourself. You can take a lunch hour to meditate or journal. Take some time with a friend to assess your lives, or do a two-minute deep breathing retreat.

How you structure your personal retreat isn't as important as the intention of a retreat. The point is to take time, in some way, form, or fashion, to revisit yourself. For me, in my life, my office is created to be one of my spaces for retreat. When I walk into it, there are candles, and pictures, and music, things that I love, and big overstuffed chairs. It is my safe, quiet space.

Don't have a room of your own? That's okay. Maybe it's the rocking chair on your front porch, maybe it's the bench down at the park. Remember what's most important is the intention. Say to yourself, "I'm going to pull away and designate this time and this place to being conscious, thoughtful, and loving about who I am, what I want, and what I'm going to do."

POWERFUL QUESTIONS:

When do you stop moving and doing? Where do you find the
peace and quiet to be with yourself to hear your life speak?

What are some of the signs that you recognize in your
own life that make you think that you need to retreat? In
what ways would retreating be beneficial in your life?

What ways can you think of to introduce
mini-retreats into your life?

*"To be guided by your inner wisdom,
you have to stop moving, stop doing,
and listen to yourself."*

– MAYA ANGELOU

"When we learn how to listen more deeply to others,
we can listen more deeply to ourselves."

– PARKER PALMER

Life design work can certainly be done alone, but working together with others can be a lot more fun. Sharing - talking out loud and listening - whether with another person (a friend or a professional) or in a group or a circle, opens up a dialogue and provides a sense of connection. We see ourselves in each other's eyes. We grow when we are in deep, meaningful contact with others.

I have been facilitating women's circles, programs, and retreats for many years now and have experienced the power that happens when people come together for healing and growing purposes. In these relationships, we come together for the intention of supporting each other. Circles can be 2 people or 10 people, and can be formal or not. It is the intention for the time together that is important.

Circles are healing and sacred relationships, because they are based in truth, honesty, and support. When we share with others, we honor certain commitments in order to promote the sense of safety and support necessary for intimate inner work. For example, at the beginning of a retreat, I ask each participant to commit to confidentiality and to make a promise that all information shared will stay within the group. For people to share deeply, they need to feel safe.

You can do this on an intimate level too, with a friend, by simply asking and assuring that what is discussed will remain confidential. You also want to agree not to be critical or to offer unsolicited advice. Offering opinions and feedback are different than offering advice. One way to be sure is to ask, "Would you like to know what I hear, and what other options I see?"

And there's no place for criticism. Criticism is a real roadblock to growth. People grow when they feel accepted and nurtured, when they feel safe being who they are, and don't have to fear rejection or criticism. In this special relationship, we listen without judgment. We agree to hold the space for each of us to explore our lives.

The last commitment is to honor each other. We honor that everyone's story is our story, and that in hearing each other's stories, we heal and we grow. In a sharing relationship, we choose to be heart-centered and committed to fostering a safe and supportive climate for self and others. We give and receive feedback and share ideas. Together we create a space for growth.

"A safe circle holds the dream and nourishes the possibility."

– JEAN SHINODA BOLEN

POWERFUL QUESTION:

When you choose to share your story with someone,
what do you want from them? What would you
ask for…confidentiality? Feedback? Silence?

"What is REAL?" asked the Rabbit one day, when they were lying side by side near the nursery fender, before Nana came to tidy the room. "Does it mean having things that buzz inside you and a stick-out handle?"

"Real isn't how you are made," said the Skin Horse. "It's a thing that happens to you."

"Does it hurt?" asked the Rabbit.

"Sometimes," said the Skin Horse, for he was always truthful. "However, when you are Real you don't mind being hurt."

"Does it happen all at once, like being wound up," he asked, "or bit by bit?"

"It doesn't happen all at once," said the Skin Horse. "You become. It takes a long time. That's why it doesn't often happen to people who break easily, or have sharp edges, or who have to be carefully kept. Generally, by the time you are Real, most of your hair has been loved off, and your eyes drop out and you get loose in the joints and very shabby. But, these things don't matter at all, because once you are Real, you can never be ugly, except to people who don't understand."

– THE VELVETEEN RABBIT

Doing personal growth work requires courage, honesty, and a willingness to be vulnerable - to be real. But what does it mean to be real? Being real means acknowledging all of the parts of ourselves—the good, the bad and the ugly. To be real means to be all of who you are. *To be real means to tell the truth.* As intimidating as that might be, the payoff is worth it.

Not being a literary scholar, imagine my surprise when I learned that one of my favorite authors, George Eliot, was actually Mary Ann Evans. Mary Ann Evans used a male pen name both to be taken seriously and also to shield her private life from public scrutiny. She lived her entire life inauthentically in order to be taken seriously and to be emotionally safe. Sound familiar to anyone?

I had a client tell me just recently that she still finds herself holding back in intellectual conversations, so that she doesn't risk sounding foolish or argumentative. Even though she is bright and articulate, she learned very young that to be emotionally safe, she needed to be polite...and quiet. Sound familiar?

How many of us hide our true natures, who we really are, in order to be safe, to feel protected, to be taken seriously? While there are obvious reasons for why we hide our true selves, there is always a price to pay. And each and every one of us knows it. We've paid it over and over, many times, in many ways in our lives.

Living authentically is no easy business—at least not in the beginning. (I promise you, it gets easier the more you do it.) Speaking our truth about who we are and who we aren't, what we value, what we think, what we believe, what we want and what we don't want, requires a great deal of self-awareness and courage.

When I grew up, it wasn't safe to be sensitive and vulnerable. I'm sure this was true for many people. It was very important to be tough. "Don't wear your emotions on your sleeves." "Don't let them see you cry." So I learned how to appear very tough and unaffected, hiding my feelings behind my intellect.

But the truth about me is that I am deeply sensitive and emotional, and things/people can hurt me very much at times. Telling this truth not only makes me vulnerable, it also makes me not fit in with the culture of my family. But it is a truth about who and how I am. I have learned to embrace it and to stand up for it. I have learned that safety lies in trusting *me* to love and support *me*. Also, with great delight, I now find that one of the reasons most people are attracted to me is because they appreciate that I am deeply sensitive and emotional.

To do this work, you have to be willing to tell the truth. While it may be scary at first, there is great emotional freedom that comes with saying, "The truth about me is…." Here's the payoff; you get to be real. Your inner world finally begins to match up with your outer world and you are living in alignment.

Speak your truth, even if only to your journal, then embrace and celebrate yourself for all of who you are. If you need a shot of courage, remember the beautiful line from *The Velveteen Rabbit*, when the Skin Horse says,

"Once you are real, you can never be ugly…"

POWERFUL QUESTIONS:

What is one piece about myself I have been hiding,
denying, resisting, so that I could be safe?

Finish this sentence, "The truth about me is…"

When or where or with whom are you most likely not to be real?

This is not simply about wanting.

This is about the power of living your life with intention. Imagine if every time you said "I want _____," instead you said "I intend _____." For example, instead of saying "I want a peaceful life," you say "I intend to be peaceful in my life." Say it out loud. Notice the difference. Can you feel the power shift?

Being intentional requires being very conscious and deliberate about what you want and how you intend to be. Don't confuse intentions with goals. An intention is about the experience you want to have, not about what you mean to accomplish. It's the mindset - the *how*, not the *what*, or the *why*. "I want to lose 15 pounds" isn't an intention, it's a goal. An intention would be, "I intend to be mindful, self-accepting, and deliberate about my diet." Again, feel the power shift.

The practice is to get very intentional about how you want to be as you go through the life design process and your life. For example, set the intention to be thoughtful, loving, and compassionate as well as constructive, as you explore your life. Some more examples are: Have an intention for how you want to be when you talk to your family. Have an intention for how you want to experience a walk or an outing. Have an intention to be loving and peaceful to yourself and others. Live your life intentionally.

Intentions keep us focused on what it is that we want to experience or realize. Intentions let the unconscious know what to expect. Intentions are the instructions that set the stage for how you are going to live your life. Being intentional is scientifically proven to have a positive effect on outcome. And while that may sound a bit supernatural, it's really about directing the Reticular Activating System of the brain. The RAS is the part of the brain that decides where we focus our attention and where we don't. Setting intentions will wake your RAS up to what you want it to pay attention to.

Writing also triggers the RAS, which then sends a signal to the cerebral cortex; "Wake up! Pay attention! Don't miss the detail!" Once you put something in writing, whether it's a goal, a desire, a dream, or an intention, your brain will begin working overtime to see that you get it, and will alert you to the signs and signals that you might have otherwise missed.

This is a beautiful intention statement that you could use to begin every day of your life. I use it every time that I get to be in a circle with others.

Today I intend to let everything be whatever it is.

Today I intend to judge nothing and nobody nor myself.

Today I will intend to see myself and all others as we truly are.

Today I will listen for the sweetness of my mind, the softening of my heart, the stillness in my body, and the serenity of my spirit.

Today I intend to listen to my life and sing my song.

Powerful Question:

What's your intention for reading this book?

"It is a commonly held view that meditation is a way to shut off
the pressures of the world or of your own mind,
but this is not an accurate impression.
Meditation is neither shutting things out nor off.
It is seeing things clearly, and positioning yourself
differently in relationship to them."

– JON KABAT-ZINN

Have you ever stood back and watched the way your mind goes? It's a horrible taskmaster; mine certainly can be. Sometimes my mind has my mother's voice, and sometimes my mind has society's voice, and sometimes my mind has the voice of my anxieties. Meditation frees us up to step back and get a little distance from all of that noise.

The key to this empowerment tool is to have the willingness to understand that our mind is not who we are. If we can learn to silence the mind, if we can learn to *witness* the mind, we can then make a more meaningful connection with ourselves, others, and our higher power.

Meditation is designed to help you reach that deeper place within yourself, from which you can bring forth new revelations and visions, deeper insights and healing, greater love and peace. The gifts of this inner life are like buried treasure, waiting to be unearthed and carried up into the light.

How do you meditate? There is no one way. Some people take it as a real discipline and a spiritual practice. Some people consider rocking on their front porch with a cup of coffee a meditation. And for those of us who like a strict practice and a "step one, step two" type of thing, there are eight trillion books and articles on the Internet to guide you. My meditation practice is putting on a special piece of music that I have, and sitting in my chair for twenty minutes every morning. I try to see if I can find an empty space that lets me see what I call the beautiful blue sky of Heaven.

There's nothing mysterious about meditation. You don't have to get into the lotus position. For most people, however, setting aside a regularly scheduled time for meditating is very helpful. Maybe you want to establish a goal of meditating for twenty minutes twice a day. Whatever your schedule or practice, I suggest that it's a gentle form of self-discipline. Some days you may only meditate briefly, or you may skip it altogether.

Remember, it's the intention, not the discipline that will take you where you want to go. If you take three minutes, and three deep breaths—that's a meditation practice. The point is, it's invaluable. Whatever way you end up doing this, learning to meditate will change your life. It's about learning to recognize that your mind is a tool which you can learn to use for your good, instead of letting it drive the car. All you have to do is—stop and be silent.

Quiet the chattering of your mind, and breathe…breathe… breathe…and repeat…breathe, breathe, breathe.

POWERFUL QUESTION:

How could you incorporate meditation into your life?

CREATING A SPACE, TOOL #7: JOURNALING

"Sometime in your life you will go on a journey.
It will be the longest journey you have ever taken.
It is the journey to find yourself."

– KATHERINE SHARP

This empowerment tool comes right after meditation for a reason. Some days I can't shut my mind off, but it's a fascinating thing just to watch the craziness that's going through it, which is why I always partner a little journal writing right after I sit still.

If you don't know who you are or what you want, start writing. Writing helps you build an intimate relationship with yourself. It lets things bubbling around in the soup of your unconscious rise to the top, where you can get a good look at them. I call this journaling yourself home.

There are so many benefits to using writing as a personal growth tool. Whether you're writing to work through your fears and anxieties, or writing your gratitude prayers, or just making lists, writing has a way of bringing substance to our thoughts and feelings. It has a way of making them real and tangible. I hear some of you muttering, "But I can't write." Push past it. Trust me, the rewards will be well worth the initial discomfort

It's also a powerful manifestation tool; by writing down your goals, desires, and dreams, you activate an inner magnet that draws those things from the universe to you. And it's a healing tool; you can write yourself through to resolution on the issues in your life, and give yourself the gift of insight and clarity.

Choose a quiet time to write, a time when you're less likely to be interrupted. It's a great way to begin and end the day, by refocusing on yourself and your inner world. You'll be amazed at what you discover.

Everyone has her own approach to journaling. I like to journal with a split page. On one side of the page I write all the craziness, and on the other side of the page I ask my "wise voice"—the voice that loves me, cares for me, believes in me— to look at what I just wrote. And it helps me. When I go into an out-of-balance place in my life, invariably, it's when I've stopped writing. That's how powerful the tool of journaling is for me. Again, all of these things will be different for different people, but if I had to choose my most important empowerment tool, it's journaling. Make it one of yours.

Throughout this book you will be invited to write—a lot. Use your journal to record your thoughts and feelings, dreams and desires, plans and goals, and commitments to your life. As with meditation, there is no one correct way. Follow your stream of consciousness and write whatever comes to your mind without censoring yourself. For myself, I prefer a free form of writing. But I also like being asked powerful questions to prompt my journal writing. I like the structure and guidance that comes from a process and from someone else being on the journey with me.

Writing saved my soul. Writing helped me find my sanity. It continues to help me. It helps me to find my voice, my true self, my inner knowing and guidance, my truth, and my wisdom. Use this tool! Write every day. Learn to trust yourself and write whatever comes to mind.

And why do we write?
We write to tell our truth.
We write to know who we are.
We write to find our voices.
We write to save the world.
We write to save ourselves.
We write so that when we look back
And see that moment when we are
Totally clear, completely brilliant
And astoundingly wise,
There is proof —
Proof right there on the page.

– **NANCY SLONIM ARONIE,** *Writing from the Heart*

POWERFUL QUESTION:

What do you want/need to be writing about in your life?

*"I have never known any distress that an
hour's reading did not relieve."*

— CHARLES DE MONTESQUIEU

It's tremendously reassuring to know that, whatever you're going through, however difficult your process may be, others have been there before you. Their wisdom is there for you. And when I'm in that space in my life when I can't pull up any wisdom on my own, where the snakes are just running amuck in my head and I can't see daylight to save my soul, that's when I reach out for the writings and the music that inspire and help me.

Some day I just might write a memoir that's about what was going on in my life at its lowest points, and what I read during those times that helped me.

The first self-help book I read was *I'm Okay, You're Okay*, and when I read it, it was like the light bulb went off. I got it. Then I read Wayne Dyer's first book, *Your Erroneous Zones*, and it was like, zap! And when I read *Return to Love*, by Marianne Williamson, the power in what she said was inspiring. That book genuinely changed my life.

There's a list at the back of this book of writings and music that I've found so helpful in my own life and work. I hope you'll take the time to sample some of these insightful, inspirational works for yourself. My massive use of quotes in this book is testimony to how important other's words of wisdom have been to me. You will see that I have some favorites like Marianne Williamson and Parker Palmer. You'll find your own favorites.

When I need help, I know where to go in my library to find what I need. In fact, with *Return to Love* I've gone through the book and made a whole file, and typed it up so I don't have to leaf through the book anymore. I can just pull a page out of my file and read it. On those days when I can't seem to find any wisdom in my own heart at all, I'll read it. Create your own library.

And there's always music. I've told you how I use music to help me meditate, to help me quiet my mind. And if you come to one of my retreats, you'll find that music is a major tool. We use poetry. We use readings. We use music. All of these are portals to take us to another place where we can look at our lives. And it's not looking at our lives in a fairytale kind of way, but looking at the reality of our lives. Find your books, find your songs, and make your own list. Know where to go when you need the solace and insights that others can bring you. It's an important empowerment tool.

"Music expresses that which cannot be said and on which it is impossible to be silent.

– VICTOR HUGO

POWERFUL QUESTION:

What is the most inspiring book you have ever
read? What about it inspired you?

"If the only prayer you said in your whole life
was, 'thank you,' that would suffice."

– MEISTER ECKHART

While we're thinking about what we want, it's important to remember what we already have. Before your feet hit the ground in the morning, the first words out of your mouth and in your heart should be "thank you." Take time every day to be grateful. Pay attention to all of the gifts you've been given.

Do a gratitude journal. Every one of my journal entries ends with "thank you, thank you, thank you." Be thankful for what you are yet to receive. This activates the law of attraction. This is a tremendously important tool that we have in our box.

Begin your day by being grateful and end your day by being grateful. Begin right now by getting very quiet, peaceful, and still. Say "thank you" for every experience of your life. Say "thank you" in advance for the glorious future you have before you. Just say "thank you."

"Let us rise up and be thankful, for if we didn't
learn a lot today, at least we learned a little."

– BUDDHA

POWERFUL QUESTION:

Describe a gratitude practice that you could do, one
that you could do daily. Is this a possibility?

"If you have built castles in the air,
that is where they should be.
Now put the foundations under them."

– HENRY DAVID THOREAU

Your Foundation

N ow that you have some tools, let's begin. Building the foundation of your life design starts with asking and answering the first most powerful question: Who Am I? Really? The blueprint for your home, the vision for your life, as well as your next steps, will grow from this core exploration.

In a world rampant with makeovers, my client Meredith was very clear that she was not interested in making herself over or changing herself into something that she wasn't. She simply wanted to be living her life according to who she already was. This was not to be a makeover. But, who was she?

She had lost touch with the foundation of who she was as a child, as well as who she was now, as a person, a soul and a spirit. She had no clue about what was true for her anymore.

For reasons with which we're all too familiar, she had changed herself to fit the demands of others and what she thought she had to do to make it in this world.

Most of the time in personal growth work, you hear about self-discovery. I say re-discovery because I believe most of us are simply trying to get back to our essential nature, the true self that we've either lost or never knew in the first place. Our vision for ourselves, if we even have one, is limited. However, now we are feeling the gap, we are experiencing the longing and the yearning of our souls.

We are all capable of so much more for our lives, and WE KNOW IT!

Just as we know that there is much more beneath the visible tip of an iceberg, we know there is much, much more to us. Rediscovery is an inner journey down into the unconscious, under the "water line" to the expansive part below the tip of the iceberg, for the purpose of bringing more of who we are up to the light.

"Who you are is so much more than what you do.
The bare and bold truth of you does not lie in your to-do list.
You are not the surface of your skin.
You are not your boundless energy.
Or your bone-wearing fatigue.
Delve deeper…"

—MARIANNE WILLIAMSON

POWERFUL QUESTION:

Are you ready to delve deeper to see who you really are?

Who are You?

There's a reason that the most dreaded interview question is, "Tell me about yourself."

When you're asked, "Who are you? Tell me about yourself" what happens? This can be an unsettling question. Some of us have shied away from this question because what we usually heard was, "*Just who do you think you are?*" And it wasn't meant to be positive.

Your sense of who you are plays a huge, interactive role in what you attract and manifest into your life. It is your major source of personal power. Knowing who you are and what you value is particularly important in today's society because everything and everybody is trying to tell us who and how we should be. So, if you aren't clear and awake, you could very well end up living someone else's life. Remember, when you know yourself, no one else can tell you who you are. Think about it.

The good news is that you really already do know who you are. If you are not in touch with it, don't worry; it's in you. You can find it. Do the work of digging the foundation of your new home by remembering who you really are. Find the power that comes from naming, acknowledging, claiming and celebrating all of who you are. Do all of the following exercises. Answer all of the questions. Use the tools you have for creating a safe space. Mainly, don't forget to write it down! Keep a record of your work.

The purpose of the following core values exercise is to help you gain awareness about what calls your name, about what is important to you. You may want to go back and review the tools for creating a space and select some, or even all of them, to use while doing this deep and personal inner work. Retreat into the stillness, be intentional, meditative and certainly use inspirational music. Then, listen and let your wisdom help you.

A commitment to turning your vision inward
on a regular basis
will train you to look inside for answers.
When you do,
You'll begin to make the highest choices for your life.
By engaging in activities
that draw you closer to yourself,
you not only create a strong attachment
to your inner world,
you learn that you can trust yourself
to handle any situation.
A solid, positive relationship with yourself
is essential.
There are no shortcuts, no quick fixes,
and no easy antidotes.
The journey to self-confidence and courage
begins and ends with you.
— CHERYL RICHARDSON, *Stand Up For Your Life*

Design Sheet #3:
Re-Discovering Your Core Values

First, quickly glance at the words, just skimming them. Pay attention to which ones seem brighter or may be jumping out at you. Next ponder the words and circle all the ones that call your name. Don't question your choices. Circle as many as you like.

Abundance	Accomplishment	Achievement
Adventure	Affection	Beauty
Belonging	Challenge	Commitment
Community	Close Relationships	Competence
Competition	Confidence	Contentment
Creativity	Curiosity	Effectiveness
Excellence	Excitement	Exploring
Family	Friendship	Harmony
Health	Honesty	Integrity
Intimacy	Job Tranquility	Joy
Knowledge	Pleasure	Public Service
Recognition	Personal Development	Reputation
Respect	Security	Serenity
Sharing	Spirituality	Strength
Structure	Success	Surroundings
Tranquility	Trust	Truth
Understanding	Uniqueness	Variety
Wealth	Well-Being	Others

Choose your top twelve words—in no particular order. You can even add some if you'd like.

1. _____

2. _____

3. _____

4. _____

5. _____

6. _____

7. _____

8. _____

9. _____

10. _____

11. _____

12. _____

Now comes the fun part of the process. Just at this moment, the sky parts open and THE POWERS THAT BE come down from the heavens, and command, "You must eliminate four of the things you value. No discussion. You must do it."

Most people do it begrudgingly. Now THE POWERS THAT BE say "You must eliminate four more." Feel this. People start getting the idea now that they are going to be asked to let go of these things, these parts of themselves.

One more time, "YOU MUST eliminate two more," then, at last, one more. Your last standing value. By this time, people are sweating, they are engaged, they have experienced making choices about who they really are.

Finally, list your final top four core values:

1. _____

2. _____

3. _____

4. _____

I love doing this process with groups of people. Now, you have some values that you can name, claim, acknowledge and celebrate!

You clearly see your attachments. After the elimination process, people are surprised and enlightened with what they can easily let go of, and what they can't seem to let go of at all. Immediately you can see the dilemmas you have with all of the daily choices you must make. We have so many competing roles and values, and every day we're expected to re-prioritize which of them to "wear." No wonder we lose touch with our genuine selves.

Note: Make copies of this Design Sheet because this is an exercise you may want to repeat as time goes by. Also, you can change the words and make an entirely new list. A powerful tool to use here is sharing. In the retreats I facilitate, we put our last four words on our nametags that we wear all weekend. We introduce ourselves to each other by talking about our words, our core selves.

Now you are truly on the journey and gathering all the tools and knowledge you are going to need to build your house. Remember your core values — your four words — as you will want to use them to design the blueprint for your most possible, fulfilling life and when you are making choices for your next steps.

"It's about making wise choices
among the things
we now have to choose from."
— **ELAINE ST. JAMES**

POWERFUL QUESTION:

With soft eyes, take a look at your life. How do these values show up in your day-to-day living? Looking at your life from the outside, could one see that these are the things that are important to you? How could you use this self-knowledge in building your life design?

There are many more exercises to help you become more aware of who you are and how you want to be. Take the time to reflect, and share, and journal about all the powerful questions you're asking and answering.

Writing your own introduction is also a wonderful exercise. Write with clarity about who you are, what's important to you, where you've been, what you're doing and why you're doing what you're doing, as well as what your dreams are. Then introduce yourself, or imagine yourself being introduced. Being a speaker and a presenter, I am constantly being introduced. Most of the time I write my own introduction. Then, I get to hear it read. Imagine the sense of affirmation and confirmation from hearing out loud who you are, what you want and what you have of value to offer.

Or you can write an ad for the personals (strictly for academic purposes, of course). I stumbled on this exercise when I was helping my mom craft a personal ad for herself. I admit I found it challenging to write a date ad for my mom— "73-year-old WWW seeking romance." However, she didn't have any problems with it. She reeled off her virtues and desires as if they were committed to memory. But really, it was because, at 73, she knew who she was and what she wanted.

One of the most-utilized life coaching exercises is to write your own eulogy. It may seem a bit morbid, but it's highly effective. If you were to die today, what would people at your funeral say about you, about your life, your accomplishments, what you stood for? It would have to be honest and accurate. Is there something you wish people could say was true about you, but it's not? Not yet?

Now let's say I tell you that you have five, or even ten more years before you are going to die. With this advanced notice and having the gift of time in which to prepare, what would people now be able to honestly say at your funeral? What would be the difference between today's eulogy and the eulogy of the future? Stop and think about it. How would you be different if you knew you were going to die soon?

The powerful question here is, what do you want to be remembered for?

She shopped well? She kept a clean house? He made a lot of money or he didn't? No, it's the significant stuff that we want to be remembered for. It's love, caring, appreciation, and kindness. We want the things we value the most to be seen in our lives.

I had the honor of delivering the eulogy at my father's funeral. This is where I got the opportunity to talk about who my father really was. Yes, he was a father and a husband and a politician and a retired naval officer and more. But I got to talk about the important stuff. In essence, this is what I said, "Because of my father, I know what it feels like to be loved—to be loved without the shadow of a doubt." This was the gift he brought to everyone in his life. What a legacy!

These exercises shine a light on some of the gaps in your life, some of the qualities you have yet to express. They give you information for designing your life. Now that you have this new self-knowledge, what will you do differently, given 10, 20, or 30 more years for your life? Use these types of exercises to help you identify your values, desires, yearnings, and maybe even your mission in life.

From this day forward, ask yourself — what do you want to stand for? It's never too late to ask these powerful questions and begin to live your answers.

POWERFUL QUESTION:

What do you want to be remembered for?

As an infant,
you were pure potential,
full and whole, open and authentic,
good and bad, disciplined and spontaneous,
a container of possibilities.
In growing up,
you disowned parts of your being
that conflicted with emerging values.
You became "this" but not "that."
By illuminating your shadow, you also reclaim your light,
You become whole again.
You become REAL.

– DEBBIE FORD

A young woman in my PeaceSeekers group was genuinely scared to take a hard look at herself. She was afraid of what she might see; perhaps traits that she couldn't accept or wouldn't like. She knew there were many things about herself that she was hiding; things she feared were ugly and disturbing. So, she simply never went there. She never went to her deeper inner place because of the dark shadows that lingered there.

Jung called that dark recess the shadow self; that part hiding in each of us that we think we'd be better off without, that we're ashamed of, that we try to hide. But the shadow self can also be a beautiful and precious piece of who we are, deep within; a part which, as children, we were often warned not to let show. For example, many women have repressed into their shadow just how powerful they really are.

All of who we are, is worthy of our awareness. You want to be whole. Trying to grow without dealing with your shadow side is like trying to walk through a dark room filled with furniture. You're bound to run into something, sooner or later. Turn on the light. Now's the time to take a look at those pieces of yourself and your experiences that you reject, hide, or deny.

What happens when we shine a flashlight in the dark corners of ourselves and really look at our shadows? Like scary monsters in our children's dark bedrooms, they usually disappear, or shrink, or transform into something familiar. Each shadow that we illuminate and integrate into ourselves allows us to move closer and closer to all of who we are, and thus toward our most authentic self.

Seek out opportunities to look deeper into yourself. Take a deep, honest look at those pieces of yourself, those experiences/thoughts/feelings that you reject, hide, or deny. Ask people close to you to point out in a loving and caring way some traits they see. Look for the use of defense mechanisms, like projection or the overuse of rationalization. A good example of projection is when someone says that she "can't stand Susan because she's a gossip." Gotcha! Who's the gossip? Those things that irritate us the most about others are very often true about us, and that's why they bother us so much.

Acknowledge your inner fear about how self-centered you can truly be, how incessant and negative the voices are in your head, how you struggle in your inner and outer life. When we acknowledge and own these parts of ourselves, we no longer need to use up our energy to keep them hidden. We are both *this* and *that*. How refreshing it is to be able to honestly say, "Yes, I am both happy and sad." "Yes, sometimes I am very depressed." Embrace all of who you are. (You will definitely want to use all of your tools for creating a safe space when you are doing shadow work.)

The Guest House

This being human is a guest house.
Every morning a new arrival.

A joy, a depression, a meanness,
some momentary awareness comes
as an unexpected visitor.

Welcome and entertain them all!
Even if they are a crowd of sorrows,
who violently sweep your house
empty of it's furniture,
still, treat each guest honorably.
He may be clearing you out
for some new delight.

The dark thought, the shame, the malice,
meet them at the door laughing and invite them in.

Be grateful for whatever comes,
because each has been sent
as a guide from beyond.

RUMI - *translated by Coleman Barks*

POWERFUL QUESTION:

What is the biggest monster in your closet?

What do you think it is that you are really afraid of?

Design Sheet #4:
YOUR MASK

Do not shrink from the opportunity to discover all of who you are, to become real and to be whole again. This exercise gives you an opportunity to explore and reveal both your mask (that part of your personality and being that you allow and want other people to see in you), and what's behind the mask (those parts of yourself that you reject or deny or repress—your darker side, or perhaps your blind side). Of course, that hidden face can also be positive.

On this side of the page (sometimes people use big index cards) write all the traits that you readily show and want others to see. For example: caring, loving, sensitive, fun-loving, and sweet.

_____

_____

_____

_____

_____

_____

_____

_____

Now, on this page (or on the back of the index card), write all the traits that you keep hidden, those parts of yourself that you reject, deny, or repress. We usually consider these to be our less attractive traits. However, they can also be positive qualities—like being smart.

_____

_____

_____

_____

_____

_____

_____

_____

_____

_____

This is a powerful opportunity to use the tool of being willing to be vulnerable and sharing. When I am working in circles with people, I ask people to read the front and the back of their cards, like this "I am…and I am also…" Claim the truth of all that you are. It will prepare you for designing a life that fits.

WHO ARE YOU? REALLY?

"Who you really are is love."

— MARIANNE WILLIAMSON

The question is not "Who are you?" but "Who are you, really?" Every time we ask *"really,"* we deepen the question, past the surface-level answers, to the essence of who we really are. All of us already use this deeper self-exploration tool every day in our lives. When we want to know the truth, we ask, "Really?" "Do you want to go that movie? Really?" Now let's use it to take us into a deeper exploration of who we think we are - really.

One of the most powerful exercises in the Women's Weekend Retreat that I facilitate is the *Who Am I, Really?* worksheet. After having done the work of creating a safe community, identifying our deepest values, maybe writing our own obituary or personal ad, and asking a lot of powerful questions, we are ready to ask the deeper question, "Who am I, really?"

Using Design Sheet #5 (page 150), women in the retreat pair up to help each other with this exploration. This exercise works best with a partner, so find someone to help you. One person asks the questions and the other records the responses. This is important because you will want this information later to help you remember. (Don't forget to use your tools to create a safe space.)

Your partner will ask your inner wisdom, "Who are you?" With reflection and heart-centeredness, you will answer. Your partner will then lean into you and gently ask you again, "But, who are you, really?" Remember to use the heart-centering tool of placing your hands over your heart to activate a heart response.

Without engaging in conversation, she will repeatedly ask you these two questions five times. Hearing the same questions asked over and over again helps you to peel back and dig deeper. Set the intentions to be real, to dream and to be brave. Seek the truth of who you really are.

"Many people who are dying
Have taken their masks off
They have come home to themselves."
— RACHEL NAOMI REMEN

Design Sheet #5:
WHO ARE YOU? REALLY?

Who are you? Really? Answer each set of questions for the purpose of digging deeper. Record and keep your responses. Write in your journal what you learned.

1. Who are you?

Who are you really?

2. Who are you?

Who are you really?

3. Who are you?

Who are you really?

4. Who are you?

Who are you really?

5. Who are you?

Who are you really?

POWERFUL QUESTION:

Imagine a newborn baby. Then remember, we each come into this world as a pure and pristine being. And underneath the layers we've accumulated, we still are. Look at a picture of yourself as a baby or small child. What do you see?

I once heard a story that each of us comes into this life as a pristine, pure, flawless diamond. And, through the trials of growing up and the course of life's pains, our innate brilliance becomes hidden by a load of rubbish.

If we are lucky, life presents us with a gift —a "wake up call." Something takes place, when for a moment we crack through the hardened surface, look past the layers of muck, and catch a glimpse of the radiant brilliance shining from deep within.

Then, if we are very, very lucky, we spend the rest of our lives journeying homeward back to this exquisite beauty and freedom. We discover that we have always been, and will always be, this pristine, flawless diamond.

This is your wake-up call, your invitation to finally come home to who you really are. You are that which you are seeking.
—BRANDON BAY, *The Journey*

"Nothing happens unless first in a dream."

– CARL SANDBURG

The Blueprint

Before you begin to build anything, you need a clear picture, a vision of what it is that you're building. You want to be able to see it in your mind's eye. Designing a blueprint requires getting back in touch with your desires, your dreams, and maybe even dreaming some new dreams. When was last time you asked yourself, what do I want? (Remember, this is not only about what you want to do or what you want to have; it is also about how you want to be.)

Of course, I'm interested in what you *really* want. In this blueprint creation stage, you will brainstorm your wants, your desires, and learn to state them as intentions. You will learn how to empower your desires by asking the deeper questions about *why* you want what you want. This process will directly link your desires to your core values.

You will also get the opportunity to work on writing a life purpose statement, as well as to daydream and visualize in every area of your life. Remember the gaps and "bumps" in your Wheel of Life? Now's the time to imagine what your world would look like if your scores were all 10's!

POWERFUL QUESTION:

Let yourself imagine what your ideal ife would look like? Describe a perfect day? What does it look like? What does it feel like?

"I can teach anybody how to get what they want out of life. The problem is I can't find anybody who can tell me what they want."

– MARK TWAIN

This is a preliminary exercise. In this step, just let yourself brainstorm a list of things you want or desire. Don't judge, analyze, or prioritize. For now, just let yourself go. The things on this list can be very concrete or abstract.

Write freely. Give yourself permission to want. If you need structure or guidance, think about the eight areas of your wheel of life and use them as a jumping-off point.

Go within and ask yourself, *what do you want?* And answer the question without censorship. No critiquing or second-guessing allowed! Speak the unspeakable; hear what your heart and soul most long for, without judgment. Consider all possibilities!

"A peaceful life comes from living in alignment with your dreams...."

Design Sheet #6:
WHAT DO YOU WANT?
GO FOR IT!

Wasn't it fun to just list your wants? I want a new car. I want to lose weight. I want to be more peaceful. I want to go to yoga. I want to be happier. And on and on. And you can have as many as you want; the more, the better. Of course, this makes some of us uncomfortable. Do it anyway! You might as well, because I am going to ask you to go even further.

Consider these next three steps to power up your wants.

1. Share your list with someone else.

2. Read your list out loud.

3. In each of your wants, strike out "I want" and replace with "I intend to." This is an amazing power shift. Remember to sit up straight when you read your new list of intentions for your life.

   (When you make the change from "I want" to "I intend," some inconsistencies will appear. I had a client one time tell me that her original statement was "I want to be a grandmother." But when she changed it to "I intend to be a grandmother," she realized that that was something out of her control.)

Next, we'll energize our desires by taking the time to look for the deeper value behind each desire that is trying to be expressed. Now we ask the very important question, but what do you *really* want?

POWERFUL QUESTION:

Do you remember what you wanted when you were a younger person? Which of your desires were fulfilled, and what are some that were not?

"...let the soft animal of your body love what it loves."
– MARY OLIVER

What Do You Really Want?

*"It doesn't interest me what you do for a living.
I want to know what you ache for and if you dare
to dream of meeting your heart's longings."*

– Oriah Mountain Dreamer

What do you really want? Most of us don't know, not really. Not what we truly desire. Growing up, most of us learned more about what others wanted for us, and from us. We felt we needed to please these others to get what we wanted, sometimes even to survive. So we invested more of our time and energy into figuring out what they wanted and how to mold ourselves to please others, than we did in figuring out what we wanted for ourselves.

Before designing a lifestyle rich in purpose, you must first know what you want. But beyond knowing what you want, you need to know why you want it. Know what pleases you. Be aware of what makes you feel alive. What is the emotional and spiritual core of what you want? The more meaning you attach to your desire, the more valuable it will be for you.

For most people, the desire to lose weight is more than about wanting to look better or even to be healthier. When we dig around this desire, we find that what most of us really want is our sense of control back in our lives. We want to feel like we are in charge and not a slave to food and bad habits. We want to feel like we can trust ourselves to live up to what we say is important.

Using Design Sheet #6 (page 156), choose your five most important wishes/wants/desires. Choose the ones that you'd like to empower and list them on Design Sheet #7 (page 161). Go through the process of asking some of the "why" questions, questions like: Why do I want that? What will that do for me, or get me in my life? What feeling will I get from this? Which value will be met by fulfilling this want? What do I really want?

Go back and revisit Design Sheet #3 (page 134). Be reminded of the values that you used then to describe yourself. Check for alignment—do your desires line up with your core values?

This is a good exercise to do with a friend. Take turns asking each other these exploratory questions using safe space tools, like willingness to be real and willingness to share. Remember to talk about confidentiality, and how to be good helpers to each other.

POWERFUL QUESTION:

What are your heart's deepest desires?

Design Sheet #7:
WHAT DO YOU REALLY WANT?

1. I want:

   The reason I want this is:

   The need/value I am trying to meet is:

2. I want:

   The reason I want this is:

   The need/value I am trying to meet is:

3. I want:

   The reason I want this is:

   The need/value I am trying to meet is:

4. I want:

   The reason I want this is:

   The need/value I am trying to meet is:

5. I want:

   The reason I want this is:

   The need/value I am trying to meet is:

"Some people have wishes, powerful people have purposes."

– WASHINGTON IRVING

Knowing your purpose can help you set your course in life. It helps us to choose goals, but life purpose is not a goal. A goal is something that can be reached. A purpose is never achieved. Purpose is a direction, like going west. No matter how far west you go, there is always still more "west" to travel. And like directions, a purpose helps you to choose your path. Your purpose is your "North Star." It can guide your life.

Every one of us has a defining piece, which is our calling; the role we are to play, the gifts we have to share, the song we have to sing. You have a calling, and each of us has been called to come forth and participate in our most possible lives.

And you have been given gifts and attributes to help you do the job - gifts and attributes that are uniquely yours. Some of us are good problem solvers, or good musicians, or caring mothers, or good friends. My husband is a good stabilizer. He is able to bring clarity and insight and direction to situations where there is conflict or confusion.

Also, purpose is not something you invent. It is something you discover. Whether you are aware of it or not, it is already there and when you are able to name it, you will recognize it and you will know that it has been there all along. Your life purpose shows up in your talents, in the things you learn rapidly and that you enjoy learning more about, the things you do superbly.

Many things give us insight into our life purpose. Simply put, your purpose can be discovered through what you're attracted to, what you're interested in, what you love and what you desire. We often find our purpose where we find our attention. We find clues to our purpose in the words or ideas that bring a tingle of excitement and hope. All of these things are clues as to what the organizing energy of our life is about.

Knowing your purpose and your deepest longings will help you in making the decisions about how you shall live. Bottom line: Life is about the choices you make. Imagine that from now on, rather than responding from old patterns, being reactive, or making choices from emotions like fear and confusion, every choice you make will be made in the light of your purpose, your values, your dreams—what you really want.

Take this opportunity to explore. Do the Life Purpose exercise (Design Sheet #8, page 164) to get a glimpse into your reason for being.

Do not miss out on this opportunity to do
the work of your life.....

Design Sheet #8:
WRITING YOUR LIFE PURPOSE

Once I worked with a fabulous life coach, (Vicki Escude, from SUN Coaching) and we're using the process below that she helped me write:

My Life Purpose Statement:

Is to use my talents and my gifts to seek and create meaningful experiences so that first I can remember who I really am, and then to help others, which will, in the end, create a healthier world for all of us.

What's yours? Why don't you try the process too?

1. Get a Partner. You'll need paper, a pen and an index card.

2. Taking turns. First Person—Remember a time in your life when you felt the most fulfilled, living completely in the moment, full of joy, and as if you were doing what you were meant to be doing in life.

   Now recount this story in detail to your partner, remembering and relishing all of the memories.

3. Partner—Write as much of the story down as possible, using your shorthand if you must.

4. When the first person has finished, the partner will retell the story to her.

5. Both storyteller and scribe will be listening for key words. Together, make a list of all the key words you both heard in the story.

   (If you feel your first story did not yield enough information, tell another story.)

6. Practice writing a sentence from the keywords.

7. Develop this sentence into a life purpose statement. Write it out on your index card.

   Work on it until it is a statement that feels true for you.

_____

_____

_____

_____

_____

The Power of a Vision

*Allow yourself to dream, to expand yourself,
to consider all the possibilities.*

I've had many, many visions in my life and no, I'm not psychic
or diagnosable! You see, we are on a journey and no one single
vision can be expected to take us through a whole life. I had
a vision of overcoming being an overweight person. I had a
second vision of earning a Ph.D. so that I could do the work
that was important to me. I had another vision of finding a
loving life partner. I had a vision of being a strong and powerful
person in my life. I also cherish a vision of myself as a soft and
compassionate person. And while there have been many twists
and turns and false starts, many of my visions- my dreams -
have been realized.

Let me teach you about the power of a vision. Envisioning
helps to make a dream a reality. While I believe in the metaphysical process in which the divine powers of the universe are
activated to answer my prayers, I also know that manifestation is a neurological process. In the back of our brains is a
section called the Reticular Activating System, the RAS, which
I talked about in an earlier section of this book. As I explained,
the function of the RAS is to consciously and subconsciously
control our attention. And the RAS can be programmed to
pay attention to specific things. Have you ever bought a blue
Honda, only to go out the next day and notice that everyone
and his brother has a blue Honda? Or, if you were trying to get
pregnant, all of a sudden it seemed as though every woman you

met was pregnant? It's not a coincidence. What is happening is that now the RAS is activated to look for these things, and you're finding what you're looking for. Holding a clear and constant vision of what you want activates the power of the RAS and you suddenly begin to see more and more things related to your dreams, thus opening more and more opportunities for fulfilling them. In the most literal and concrete way, having a vision helps you to find your dreams.

Every wisdom tradition holds that we can create our own fate, and encourages us to use our imagination to create it. Visualization accesses power that you have within you. The power of visualization has been proven to literally change physical reality. You *do* have the ability to co-create and design your life, from both a deeper and a broader level.

Have your ever imagined your most perfect day? This is a powerful envisioning activity. Use Design Sheet #9 (page 168) to design a vision in all the areas of your life. Dream your bigger life.

"To accomplish great things you must not only act,
you must dream.....and believe."
– ANATOLE FRANCE

Design Sheet #9:
VISUALIZING YOUR LIFE

In each of the following areas of your life, what are your possibilities?

Write down what you want, whatever it might be, in loving detail. Your dreams and desires are your maps to your life purpose and your destiny. These become the visions for your life.

Don't worry if you have trouble actually seeing pictures. Let the vision come to you in whatever form that it does. You may see your vision in descriptive words. You may envision your own movie or script of what your dream or desire would look like. Use as many descriptors as you can. This also helps plant the seeds of the possibility in your subconscious. Identify clearly what you want, what it would look like, and how you would feel when you had it.

Physical Well-Being:

Romance, & Intimacy:

Family:

Friends and Support System:

Work (Career & Money):

Spirituality:

Fun and Recreation:

Other: *(Choose whatever came up for you as a very special section of your Wheel of Life. Some people choose to put emotionality, or family, or physical environment. Pick what matters to you.)*

Now go back through each vision and ask yourself,
"Is this a possibility?"

Remember the importance of this single question. Drop down, into your heart and your inner guidance, and lovingly ask yourself - "Do I believe?" Then, listen. Since they have been cultivated from the heart, odds are that these are your true possibilities.

God grant me the serenity to accept the things I
cannot change; courage to change the things I can;
and wisdom to know the difference.

– THE SERENITY PRAYER

The Design

O kay—you know who you really are and you know what you really want. Now what? How do you design/build/live your life? What will be your next choices, your next steps? *Knowing This, How Then Shall You Live?* is the title of a Wayne Mueller book and is perfect for the final of *The Three Most Powerful Questions*.

Throughout our lives we are either consciously or unconsciously making choices, day-by-day and minute-by-minute. We are making the big choices and the small, next-step choices, sometimes all at the same time. We make decisions about whether we marry, have children, and where we're going to live, along with myriad other lifestyle choices. We make decisions about our professional lives, our friends and family, what we choose to believe, and our attitudes. All of these choices have shaped the person that we are now.

This Life Design worksheet (Design Sheet #10, page 184) is for helping you make empowered choices—choices that have a higher probability of getting you what you really want in life, and taking you where you really want to go. You have the tools to ask and answer hard questions like: "Is this a true calling of the heart? Am I building on rock or sand? Will this choice energize or de-energize my life? Is this my true choice, or am I trying to please someone else? Is this direction in alignment with the self-knowledge gained from the foundation and blueprint processes? Is this a possibility?"

Now's the time to begin building. Just like a home is built brick by brick, a life is built step by step. Do you know what your next steps are? The Life Design worksheet (page 184) will help you to take your goals, dreams, and desires and transform them into beliefs, choices, and action. Make your choices based on what's most important you. This is what will energize you to move forward. You will feel motivated and resourceful. You will be empowered to take your next steps.

"It's never too late..."
– George Elliott

POWERFUL QUESTION:

Knowing what I now know, am I living in alignment?

"Life is a building. Every act of our commonest
days adds to the invisible building."

– J. R. MILLER

Let's review the process so far. You were introduced to your
overall life picture with the Wheel of Life. From this exercise,
you got a quick glance at how balanced or unbalanced your
life looked. You could see gaps that needed to be filled. You
began to see the big picture. Most importantly, you began to
feel longings and the pull to grow.

Next, you went through a deep exploratory process using
powerful questions and exercises that helped you dig for the
truth of who you are and what you want...and maybe even
your Life Purpose. Take some time to revisit all of the powerful
questions, exercises, and the information on the Design Sheets
you've done so far.

After spending some time looking at all the possibilities,
choose the areas you want to work on now. You do not need
to do everything at once. Remember, this is a building project.
I would suggest that you prioritize, decide on the two or three
areas in your life that you most long for, or that are the most
significantly out of balance, and begin with them. You can go
through this process as many times as you'd like.

Working now through the Life Design worksheet (Design
Sheet #10, page 184), you'll learn how to harness the power
of your visualization by crystallizing it into an empowering

snapshot. You'll identify the negative thoughts that work against you, and learn to transform them into authentic powerful beliefs. You will come up with some concrete next steps to move you forward towards your ideal picture. But, most importantly, at every step of the process, you will learn how to drop down, access your inner wisdom and tell the truth about your possibilities.

I am going to walk you through each step of Design Sheet #10 - The Life Design Worksheet. At the end of this section is the blank worksheet for your use. Make a lot of copies. You will want to do this process over and over again. Eventually it will become your natural process for deciding your next steps. Remember what Gloria Steinham said; it's not about the content, it's about the process. Learning to take yourself through a grounded series of questions and reflections will serve you all the days of your life. Remember, you never stop growing, and you are always faced with choices.

Possibility: Something within the limits of ability, capacity or realization. Something that may or may not occur. Something that is capable of existing or happening.
– WEBSTER'S DICTIONARY

POWERFUL QUESTION:

What decision making process have you been using in your
life up until now -- or have you been living by default?

Review of the Life Design Worksheet

(Design Sheet #10, page 184)

Step 1: Visualize Your Dream

1. Choose one of your possibilities from the Visualizing Your Life exercise. Write a visualization of this possibility in loving detail. Identify clearly what you want, what it would look like, what you would feel. Paint the picture.

(Remember the power of a vision. You want to activate your RAS so it will pay attention to what you want. Visualizing is neurological as well as psychological and metaphysical. This is powerful stuff.)

From the full, radiant visualization, take a snapshot. This is a lot like putting a picture on the refrigerator door.

Snapshot Tips:

Ultimately this ought to be a single image—like a billboard or snapshot. It should:

- Be either literal or metaphoric.

- Evoke feeling.

- Include you in it.

- Be physically recorded. Write it down.

What's the snapshot picture?

(Don't worry about the gap between where you are and where you want to be. Better still, pay attention to the gap. Let this tension work for you. The human system is designed to alleviate tension in our lives. The tension helps us physiologically move toward our visions.)

Is this a possibility?

So, now that you have a powerful snapshot of your possible life in your mind's eye, here comes the most important question that you must ask yourself; *do you believe?* Do you believe that *this* vision, *this* snapshot of your life, is a possibility? Really? This is the power of the Possible Life Design process—the continual checking in with your wisdom and your commitment. This kind of clarity and honesty requires the tool of heart-centeredness; the ability to drop down and listen. This requires you to be willing to be vulnerable, to be real. Using all of your tools, drop down and ask—*is this a possibility?*

Ask your deeper self the question, "Is this desire, this vision, really a possibility? From this place, seek an answer. It may be that your powerful self resonates thoroughly with your snapshot and cries "Yes!" It may be cautious, but encouraging. The wise, inner voice, might say, "Not now" or "That doesn't really fit." (If that's the case, we just keep re-crafting our vision until it gets the green light.) We can force ourselves, pushing against the tide, but we'll end up tired and burned out. It's much better to be going with the tide, moving in the direction in which we are naturally meant to grow. Our snapshot will pull us, and eventually we will be what we never thought was possible. Remember, this is a building process.

2. Identify any limiting beliefs/thoughts you have about yourself and this desire. What is your negative, self-defeating inner dialogue?

Let yourself hear all the things you say to yourself. Stop and think about each statement. Does it energize or de-energize? Is it moving you forward, or not? Is it true? How so? What makes it true? Where's your evidence? Does this attitude or belief help you get what you want?

If your inner self talk is negative and self-defeating, come up with new beliefs. Come up with new, loving authentic, alternative inner responses. Write it out and ask yourself, is this belief in my highest good and best interest?

In the work of life design, I have observed that as soon as we are able to articulate and visualize a beautiful, courageous possibility, the ego throws everything at it. This is when all the voices of fear and self-doubt amplify. The ego can become very scared when we say we are going to try to fly. It is precisely at this point that the negative, self-defeating beliefs attack in droves. And in the past, we have succumbed to their assaults.

But if we know that this is the old pattern, we can expect it and prepare for it. We can even be grateful for the opportunity to practice. I promise you that you can break this cycle when you decide you've had enough of it. Step 2 begins the exploration of old beliefs, thoughts and patterns that have been obstacles to your dreams in the past. This process takes us step by step through how to identify, evaluate, and re-decide what we are going to choose to believe.

Is this a possibility?

Once you have written down your truest, most authentic belief you have about yourself and your dream, do you believe it? Can you own it? Here it is again, another opportunity for you to deepen your inner work. Drop down. Ask sincerely. *Listen.* Because when you believe, the magic happens.

STEPS 3 AND 4. THE PLAN

3. What in the past has prevented me from having what I want? What would I have to do differently now?

4. Brainstorm a list of things you would have to do, have to have, have to check out, have to be... to be living this vision.

I have paired these two steps together because they are both self-explorations requiring that we look back with soft eyes at what's gotten in our way in the past, and also be willing to look at what we might need for the future. This work takes a lot of courage. You want to be able to honestly and lovingly take responsibility for what you've either been doing or not been doing to help yourself grow. You also want to be able to see what your next steps could be.

This is a perfect opportunity to practice mind-mapping. Mind- mapping is a bit like going on a trip or a journey without ever actually leaving. This is a powerful envisioning process that will help you to know what you need. You can get a lot of information about what you would want to do differently, as well as information about things for you to do, to have, and ways for you to be. Let the following Oriah Mountain Dreamer exercise open your eyes.

Begin with relaxing and dropping down.

Then, let yourself focus on one thing you want to do that is not currently part of your life. Let it be something specific and concrete, and imagine in detail what it would look like. It may be meditating or exercising daily, learning something new or doing something creative, leaving a job or starting a business, or simply being more patient with those you love. Pick something that has meaning for you.

See yourself beginning this activity. Imagine the state of mind, body, and emotions ideally required. How do you want to be feeling mentally, emotionally, and physically when you start? Imagine yourself as you ideally want to be, to begin. Stay with this for a few breaths.

Now, be aware of how you are feeling mentally, emotionally, and physically at this moment. Feel the gap, if there is one, between where you want to be and where you are. Imagine two selves: one, feeling as you would ideally like to feel and the other, just as you are, perhaps more tired, less inspired, less calm, or more distracted than you want to be. Let your attention follow your inhalation and your exhalation and take a few moments to feel, without judgment, the gap between where you are and where you want to be—or think you should be—to begin.

Now imagine yourself beginning what you originally wanted to do, starting from the place you are, right now. See yourself doing it—meditating, exercising, being more patient, looking for a new job—see yourself doing something differently—just the way you are, perhaps a little tired or distracted or agitated or uninspired. Do not pull away from the way you are feeling. Let yourself relax into how things are and imagine doing what you want to do, perhaps not perfectly, not as ideally as you first imagined it, but doing it anyway. Let go with each exhalation; let yourself feel exactly how you are feeling. Give yourself permission to begin from here.

Is it a possibility?

At the end of Step 3 and Step 4 on the Life Design worksheet (page 184), you will again ask your loving, all-knowing self — are these possibilities? "Is it possible that I can stop sabotaging myself with the same old obstacles, or is it possible that I will choose to do the things I know to do differently?" Keep working until you get to YES!

STEP 5. NEXT STEPS

5. *What are you willing to do? What is the next action step?*

Is it a possibility?

From the insights and information you've gathered so far from the worksheet, you can now begin to create that "to-do" list that we humans love so much. However, this "to-do" list is supercharged. It comes from the deepest part of our dreams and our possibilities. Use the Life Design worksheet in each of the following areas of your life, allowing your next steps to come forth. This model of life design is a bit different in that we just want to focus on next steps. That's because next steps are usually doable. We looked at the bigger picture in the blueprint stage, but in the action stage, we are just concerned with possible next steps.

Another important difference in this approach is that usually you are asked "what will you do?" I ask "*What are you willing to do?*" Feel the difference. We all know that, no matter how great the idea, it's not worth anything if we don't feel willing to do it. Of all of your next steps, which ones are true possibilities and probabilities for you? What next steps you are willing to take?

After you have completed the Life Design Worksheet, use Design Sheet #11 (page 188) to record the next steps in your life that you are willing to take. Let this be what guides the choices you make every day. If you stay on track and keep moving in the direction of your heart's desire, you will end up living the life you are meant to live.

As always, with each next step that you have acknowledged that you are willing to take, don't forget to ask yourself, "Is this a possibility?"

"True life is lived when tiny choices are made.
Tiny choices mean tiny changes.
But it is only with infinitesimal change,
So small no one else even realizes you're making them,
That you have any hope of transformation."

— LEO TOLSTOY

Design Sheet #10:
LIFE DESIGN WORKSHEET

(Use this worksheet for every possibility.)

1. Choose one of your possibilities from the Visualizing Your Life exercise. Write a visualization of this possibility in loving detail. Identify clearly what you want, what it would look like, what you would feel. Paint the picture.

   What's the snapshot picture?

   Is this a possibility?

2. Identify any limiting beliefs/thoughts you have about yourself and this desire. What is you negative, self-defeating inner dialogue?

Let yourself hear all the things you say to yourself. Stop and think about each statement. Does it energize or de-energize? Is it moving you forward, or not? Is it true? How so? What makes it true? Where's your evidence? Does this attitude or belief help you get what you want?

If your inner self-talk is negative and self-defeating, come up with some new beliefs. Craft for yourself some new, loving, authentic, alternative inner responses. Write them out.

Is this a possibility?

3. What in the past has prevented me from having what I want?

   What would I have to do differently?

   Is this a possibility?

4. Brainstorm a list of things you would have to do, have to have, have to check out to be living this vision.

   Which ones are possibilities?

5. What are you willing to do? What is the next action step?

Is it a possibility?

Design Sheet #11:
SOME POSSIBLE NEXT ACTION STEPS

Health and Fitness:

Romance and Intimacy:

Family:

Career and Money:

Fun and Recreation:

Spirituality:

Friends and Support System:

Other:

Rebecca began her Possible Life work in the loving community of a retreat. Afterward, she became an individual coaching client. We've known each other for a while. It's been an amazing journey. She liked the metaphor of singing her song and felt like she had a song to sing, yet couldn't remember it. On the journey, she rediscovered her love, first of all for herself, and also her love for being creative. She had forgotten.

During the retreat, after doing the work of searching core values and digging deeper for who she really was, underneath all the garbage, she was able to read out loud both the front and the back of her mask. This was the beginning of Rebecca standing up for her life.

She told me after doing the Wheel of Life Exercise that her life wasn't out of balance, it was flat. All areas were low on the satisfaction scale. She was able to see lots of room for growth, and specific areas that she could work on in her life. For the worksheet, she chose to work in the "fun and recreation" area, because her inner wisdom was very clearly telling her that if she would lighten up and have some fun, creativity would flow again. Sounded great, and felt divinely inspired! This was the possibility she wanted to work on.

She dug in and did all the exercises. She let herself dream again about what she really wanted. She designed the following visualization:

The ideal image of fun and recreation in my life is me with a light heart and a carefree nature. I see myself laughing, smiling, and relaxed. I am actively involved in activities and groups that are for the sole purpose of social and recreational fun. I am excited about initiating, and planning events for me and others.

The snapshot she designed was one of her playing in the ocean with family. She was healthy, laughing, and having fun. She posted this on the proverbial refrigerator of her mind. When asked to answer from the heart, "Is this a possibility?" her "yes" came easily and quickly. She knew she was on the right path.

In Step 2, she listened for all the negative self-defeating chatter that began immediately. Thoughts like "You're kinda old for that." "Who do you think you are?" "You're not fun." We all know the script. The negative, hurtful, self-sabotaging things we say are actually quite universal. We all do it. Rebecca's were no different. However, she stopped and took the time to evaluate all of this inner chatter. She slowed it all down and looked at it with loving eyes, looking for the truth. She was able to identify her most dangerous belief, and to do the work of dismantling and replacing it.

Rebecca worked very hard and replaced an old inaccurate belief: That she was not a fun person - that she was boring and an old fuddy-duddy (her words, not mine) with a new alternative belief, which was "I *am* fun-loving and fun to be with. I constantly seek to have fun throughout as many of my life experiences as possible." Again, when asked if there were a pos-

sibility for her to hold this new belief, she nodded confidently
and convincingly, "Yes."

With painful truthfulness, she named and took responsibility for the things that she had allowed to get in her way in
the past. In addition to her negative self talk about not being
any fun, she also focused too much on work, on chores, and on
doing things perfectly. There seemed to be no extra time for
fun and recreation. She realized that she would have to make
fun a priority and a commitment, and then plan some next
steps for it.

Rebecca was able to see the next steps almost magically
unfolding for her, not only things that she needed to do, but
also attitudes she needed to hold. She knew how she wanted
to feel and how she wanted it all to look. She now had an
empowered "to-do" list: There was a local Ski Club she could
join for free. She made arrangements for game night at her
home with friends. She actually went to the beach! Her biggest
"to-do" was to keep her thoughts, attitudes and beliefs clean
and pure of all negativity. All of these were possibilities for
her to do right now, in order to begin her growth in the right
direction - the direction of her dreams. Most importantly, they
were things she believed were possibilities and things that she
was willing to do.

"What lies behind us and what lies before us pales in comparison to what lies within us."

— RALPH WALDO EMERSON

Your Power Tools

What is personal power? Personal power is about asserting yourself in your life and being actively engaged in the process of creating your experience of life. An empowered person is one who has gone through the effort to find his or her own truth and create a life vision around it, and who is then *living this dream consistently over time.*

Now that you have the dream, the vision, and the next steps, now comes the actual building. The hard labor. The heavy lifting. This is when you have to get up every morning and do it. This is when you need the power tools, the tools that help you find the focus and the energy to make higher choices all day long - choices that are in alignment with your possible life.

This is not an easy order. Where do you get the personal power needed to energize your life designs? You're going to need some more tools. I call these final tools our power tools:

- Knowing your Truth

- Commitment and Discipline

- Accountability and Support

Find out who you are, and be that.
Decide what comes first, and do that.
Discover your strengths, and use them.
Learn not to compete with others because
No one else is in the contest of being you.

Then:
Accept your own uniqueness.
See your possibilities.
Set priorities and make decisions.
Give yourself the respect that is due.

– THE DALI LAMA

Trust your desire.
Feel what you've never felt.
Think what you've never thought.
Say what you've never said.
Do what you've never done.
Wake up to new possibilities.

Remember who you are. Remember your song. Remember what you are called to do. Remember what you really want. And as Oriah Mountain Dreamer said to us earlier, "Let this knowing guide you home." Let this knowing help you build your home.

Hopefully, you now know many ways to access your inner guidance. You want to stay in touch with this valuable information. You have many tools that you can use daily to help you stay connected. I depend on journaling and then rereading what I wrote, looking for the wisdom. I also have learned to be silent, and in the stillness to listen for the voice that loves me.

Learn to trust yourself...

POWERFUL QUESTION:

What's the best way for you to access your
wisdom—to remember your truth?

Power Tool #2: Commitment and Discipline

"When we have become who we are supposed to be, we will know what it is we're supposed to do. And when we remember that we are spiritual beings, we will have the courage to do it."

— Marianne Williamson

When you come to my weekend retreat, be prepared for Sunday morning. It is the culminating, peak experience of the retreat. After all the personal growth work that has gone on throughout the entire weekend, on Sunday morning, you write on a bright green, 3x5 index card what you want to commit to in your life…*now*.

Then everyone in the circle takes a turn standing in the middle of the circle to read her green card. This is an opportunity to make a personal declaration and rededication to yourself and to others. A card might say, "I stand here today committed to being a more loving person in my life. When you think of me, please see me going out of my way to do random acts of kindness, to smile at everyone, even strangers, more…" This is a testimony to the power of community. Imagine standing in the middle of a sacred circle making your declaration out loud, in front of everyone, and asking for their support.

Speaking aloud like this is an act of empowerment. Who could you make a commitment to right now? Who could witness your promises to live your own true life? This is important because this may be the first time ever that you've made this promise out loud. Take advantage of this power tool. Commitment drives discipline.

"Without inner stability,
or the right mental attitude,
one cannot be happy, calm or at peace.
This is why training the mind is imperative.
Some technique or method for training the mind
should be a part of everyone's daily life."

– HIS HOLINESS, THE DALAI LAMA

Mary Ann is a beautiful, dedicated writer. She has mastered the art of discipline in terms of her diet and fitness programs. She is slim and athletic, even at the age of 50-something. She has also mastered the self-control it takes to sit down and write every day for several hours. When I asked her how and where she acquired that discipline, she said, "I made a decision. I decided this was how I wanted to be living. That this was what was most important to me." She said then that she just began to do it, always staying focused on her decision, until the dream became a reality, a part of her everyday life. One day the dream became her actual life. She was living her ideal day.

What's important about Mary Ann's story is that she did not exercise the same discipline in other areas. Her negative, self-defeating thoughts about herself were out of control. She had ugly interior voices that said terrible things to her, and they were relentless. The moment she was able to recognize that she could use the same discipline for her mental and emotional life as she had for her physical and her writing life, she got it.

Discipline is such a huge topic. And because we feel so lacking in it we don't really want to talk about it. But talk about it we must. What happened for Mary Ann is that, first of all, she realized she was actually good at the art of discipline. She revisited how she had disciplined herself to go regularly to the gym and to write on a daily schedule.

She'd already created the necessary script for disciplining herself to make the gym and her writing routine her priorities and she had followed through with it. She now designed a plan based on the new belief that she could apply the same level of effective self-discipline in her mental and emotional life. She learned about the power of her thoughts and how to transform them. She committed to being a more light-hearted soul, free of negativity and fear. And, she committed to some next steps, and began to do what she knew she really wanted to do.

This is what discipline is; committing to and practicing something until it becomes a part of who we are naturally. Mary Ann no longer has to push herself to work out; she is now a fit person and this is just what she does. She no longer dreams of being a writer, she writes. Discipline is what turns dreams into reality.

We all have to find what works for us personally, when it comes to what motivates and inspires us. What makes us keep moving forward even when we don't want to take the next step? The work here is to recognize what Mary Ann recognized: She has the ability to be disciplined when she makes the commitment. She began to practice every day taming the negative thoughts and replacing them with empowering thoughts. Now those thoughts have created her reality, the new reality of who she is.

Do what Mary Ann did. Figure out what works for you.

POWERFUL QUESTIONS:

What rituals or practices could you use to
empower your commitments?

Who would you be willing to share your commitments with?

Think of a practice in your life, or an attitude, in which you are already highly focused and disciplined, whether it be brushing your teeth, or praying every night, or going to the gym. What did you do to develop this discipline?

Where could you use discipline today? Is this a possibility?

"Accountability breeds response-ability."

– **STEPHEN COVEY**

Being willing to be held accountable for your desires, dreams, and next steps is a powerful tool to be taken advantage of. This is the place you want to ask, "How will I hold myself accountable for doing and being what I said I wanted? How will I hold myself responsible for following through with the steps I've identified, to get what I want?"

Some people use a reward system to help them stay on track and focused. When I was in graduate school, which took a tremendous amount of time and effort, I would reward myself with a new pair of earrings every time I met a goal, each time I accomplished that next step. The earrings were just small trinkets, but they helped me to keep my eyes on the bigger prize. What will help you stay focused? What will power up your response-ability?

Having to answer to someone else gives us an extra, added dose of power and incentive to follow our dreams. Most of us do better when we've got partners in the process. Remember, sharing is a powerful tool. I'd like you to consider who you could partner with, someone who will help you to honestly hold yourself accountable.

Create a circle of powerful people around you. This is one of the most magical things you can do for yourself. There is collective power in community. Attend a retreat. Join a group.

I have been a member of Weight Watchers off and on since I was in my twenties. If I work the program, it never fails me. Weight Watchers has always been a model for me about how to help people make different choices and how to transform their lives.

The diet is a commonsense, healthy one that we all know we should be following — lots of vegetables, cutting down on sugar and smaller portion sizes — but for me it's not just the diet that makes the program so special. You also get massive amounts of information in the materials, the online programs, and the weekly classes. And you become part of a community of other people who have the same desire — to lose weight, to get healthy, and to be fit.

All of these are factors as to why the program is effective. But the most powerful piece of the Weight Watchers program is accountability. It's that weekly weigh-in. Even if I weigh-in outside of the class, I still weigh-in with an instructor. She always helps me. She's an empowerment goddess who is encouraging and believes in me. When the numbers go up instead of down, she simply asks me questions and helps me explore what my obstacles and what my possibilities are. She helps me to remember and to be accountable to my vision.

Many people find accountability by doing this work one on one, with someone like me. Find a life coach who'll work with you on a regular basis. Not only will you have someone calling on you to be accountable, you'll have an expert who can help you see through the layers of "I can't" or "I don't," to the choices you want and need to make. After the many years and many clients I've worked with, this process never gets old for me. Every life is a voyage of discovery, and a qualified life coach is one who will be eager to help you make it.

This work of transforming, becoming who we really are, is very hard. It brings up all of our issues. It brings up all of our resistances. And if we don't have someone to help us with that, odds are that the minute it starts getting tough, it may seem easier just to slide back into the old roles and old ways, limiting though they are.

"Accept responsibility for your life.
Know that it is you who will get you where you
want to go, no one else."

– LES BROWN

POWERFUL QUESTION:

Who could you invite to hold you accountable to your dreams?
An individual, a group? How would you ask them to help you?

What other kind of accountability plans could you make?

If you follow your bliss,
You will put yourself on the kind of track
That has been there all the while,
Waiting for you...
And the life you ought to be living
Is the one you will be living.

– JOSEPH CAMPBELL

Your Possible Life Design Process

O nce again, the process of life design isn't something you do just one time, then consider it finished. These tools you've acquired are ones you will need to utilize daily. Because your life continues to evolve and grow, you will want to do the Wheel of Life Exercise at least once a year. Keep your visions posted in clear view and update them as needed. Make sure that you're working from your empowered list of next steps, not just a generalized "to-do" list. Gather your support system and speak your truth, make a commitment, and ask your friend or supportive circle to hold you accountable to who you say you really are and what you really want.

From this point on, you will be making not only the lifetime decisions, but also your daily, moment-by-moment decisions based on this new, empowering self-knowledge and design. You will be living the life of your dreams.

PART IV

Building a Possible World

When I was young I wanted to change the world…

Finally, I realized that if long ago I had changed myself,

I could have made an impact on my family.

My family and I could have made an impact on our town.

Their impact could have changed the nation

And I could indeed have changed the world.

— UNKNOWN MONK, 11 AD

I V

I first began writing the manuscript for this life design model years ago when I sat alone at the end of that dirt road on a deserted island. I actually journaled, "I am writing this book for others, for myself, and to transform the world." I swear I did! That was the biggest vision I ever had, and I still have it. What I *really* want at a very, very deep level is world peace. My strategy to reach that goal is to first transform myself

Individually, you and I can change the world. How? First of all, don't try to change the world. Transform yourself. Choose to be a more peaceful and loving person leading a peaceful life. Choose peace. One of Gandhi's most popular quotes is that we must be the change we seek. If we want a more peaceful world, it is up to us. We must desire peace. We must seek peace everywhere we go and in everything we think, say, and do.

Where can you be more loving and peace-oriented in your life? And who around you could benefit from it?

Make being an instrument of peace your main goal, every day. Seek peace and harmony everywhere you go and in everything you do, and because you seek it, you are more likely to find it. When you expect to find a parking space, you are more likely to find one, rather than when you go into the parking lot saying "Oh, there probably won't be a spot here for me today." What happens is that because you believe you will find a space, you will look harder and longer. The same thing happens when we enter looking for peace and goodwill. Because you expect it, desire it, seek it, you will look harder and you will be more likely to find it.

> *"Peace I find on every corner, every bus stop,*
> *every home I visit in, because I look for it."*
> — **CHARLEY THWEATT CD**

You will also bring more peace into the world. You will smile more and smile at others—which is a gift of peace. You will have positive thoughts about yourself and others, which sends out positive energy. Energetically, it is a ripple effect; what you send out affects others. One exercise I ask my clients to do is to sit in the center of the mall, watch all the people walk by, cancel any negative or judgmental thoughts they might at other times have had about them, and instead only send them loving blessings as a fellow brother or sister.

Imagine a world where we are all in love, all the time, with everyone. There would be no wars because we wouldn't fight. There would be no hunger because we would feed each other. There would be no environmental breakdown because we would love ourselves, our children, and our planet too much to destroy it. There would be no prejudice, oppression or violence of any kind. There would be no sorrow. There would only be peace. Imagine this world.

– MARIANNE WILLIAMSON

This is the only sane choice. This takes a lot of courage because this requires that you transform yourself—not others. Of course, if you stop to think about it, we've never really been able to change others, anyway. But this kind of thinking will transform the world. It will certainly transform your world. This is the only way we are ever going to change the world—person by person, thought by thought. We can ban all the bombs on the planet, but until we banish the hatred and the lack of peace in our own hearts, they will be rebuilt. The change we are all seeking happens in our individual hearts, minds, and lives. By stopping the violence (no matter how big or how small) in your own life, you will be a peacemaker in the world.

There once was a mother and daughter. The daughter had been after the mother to take her to the beach, so the mother halfheartedly told the daughter they would go on Saturday.

Well, Saturday morning rolled around and the mother settled into her chair with her coffee to read the newspaper. The daughter, however, was insistent that the mother fulfill her promise. Finally, the mother concocted what she thought was a brilliant idea. In the newspaper, there was a large picture of a map of the world. She tore the picture into small pieces and told her daughter, "When you finish putting the pieces of the map back together we'll go to the beach." Smugly, she settled back into her chair. She heard the daughter in the kitchen, rattling around with the pieces of paper and the tape.

Very soon, the daughter returned with the map perfectly assembled. "How did you do that so quickly?" the mother exclaimed.

"It was easy," replied the daughter. "You see, on the other side of the page was the picture of a woman. All I had to do was put the person together and then the whole world came together."

This is my life's calling. When we put ourselves together, the world comes together. It is in the process of living a well-designed life, step by step, that our peace, and world peace, is found.

Thank you for allowing me to sing my song. I hope this life design process is helpful as you choose to live your most wonderful, possible life.

Let there be peace on earth and let it begin with me.

POWERFUL QUESTION:

Do you believe in your power to transform the world?

Appendix A:

A GUIDED MEDITATION FOR CONSIDERING THE POSSIBILITIES FOR YOUR LIFE

(An audio recording of this guided meditation can be found at www.kathymurphyphd.com)

This guided meditation is to help you access more of who you are by going within. The secret of this meditation is to allow yourself to go deeper—to release yourself from your rational, logical mind. You know that there is a wealth of information beneath the conscious, thinking mind, and in order to access it, you need to drop down, beneath the surface.

The main ingredient to a satisfying guided meditation is to give yourself permission and to have the intention to relax and be led. The secret is in the stillness, the quietness, and the suggestion. It's also useful to begin with progressive relaxation prior to the guided imagery. Soft music is helpful, too.

Find a comfortable position. Take a long, deep breath and let it out slowly.

Bring your attention to your breath, feeling your belly rise on the inhalation and fall on the exhalation. As you breathe out, breathe out any stress or tension or tiredness. Let it flow harmlessly onto the floor and to the earth beneath you. Let any thoughts or feelings that come, drift away with the out breath. Just keep bringing your attention back to your breath and your body.

Bring your attention to your feet. Imagine being able to breathe in light and warmth into your feet, and as you exhale, let any tension or tiredness in your feet flow harmlessly out into the ground. Feel your feet relax and soften.

Breathe into your legs and the lower portion of your body. Be aware of any tension or tiredness here, and breathe it out.

Breathe into your pelvic area, up through the lower back, and up through the spine. Breathe into all the muscles of your back, filling them with breath and exhaling all stress and tension.

Breathe into your belly and up into your chest, filling your heart and lungs with light and breath. Be aware of your rib cage rising and falling. Let the muscles around your heart relax. Breathe into any area that needs softening and let all the tension and stress in the front of your body flow out with the exhalation.

Breathe into your hands, up the arms and shoulders and through the throat and neck. Let a small sound come with the exhalation, releasing the harshness of unspoken words.

Breathe into your face. Feel the muscles of your forehead and your cheeks release any tension and tiredness with your out breath.

Be aware of your whole body. Breathe into any places that still hold tension or tiredness. Let go of the hardness of hanging on. Feel yourself being supported by the chair, by the floor and the earth beneath the floor. Let go. Breathe.

In this comfortable position, you are now deeply relaxed. Allow your rational mind to rest and open to the wisdom of your soul. You are very deeply relaxed.

Drop down, deeply within. Drop down into your heart, and breathe.

Drop down into the quiet, still place within you. Down inside the very center of your heart, the very center of love and compassion.

Take your hand and place it over your heart. As you breathe deeply, allow your heart to open from the inside.

Allow this feeling to permeate your entire being, creating a deep peace within you.

From this place, allow yourself to be aware of how you see yourself and your life.

See yourself and your life with soft eyes.

Allow yourself to notice how you feel as you look at yourself and your life.

- What do you see?

- Who are you? Really?

- Are you living your life according to what's important to you?

- What do you love?
- What did you love as a child?
- What were you dreams?
- What are your dreams today?
- What do you see for yourself in this life?
- Ask yourself, Can I have this life I so desire?

Allow yourself to see the bigger version of your life.

Allow yourself to see all the possibilities for you…

In your relationships and your family life.

- What are the possibilities for you in your work and financial life?
- What are the possibilities for your physical life?
- What are the possibilities for your social life?
- What are the possibilities for your spiritual life?
- What are the possibilities for your emotional life?

Just allow whatever images or thoughts that arise to come up and float by.

Allow yourself to just take a moment and drop down into any place inside you that needs healing.

See yourself with softer eyes. And breathe.

Know the truth about yourself. Know the truth about your power. Know the truth about all of your possibilities.

Allow this self-knowledge to rise up to your conscious awareness where it can be a part of your waking, active being.

Allow yourself to sit in this loving and compassionate vision for as long as you wish.

Appendix B:

BIBLIOGRAPHY

There is so much wisdom out there in the world. Reading from the experiences and insights of others is often helpful on our journeys. And there are many, many resources. Here are some of the books that provided me with inspiration in developing this program, and which you may want to explore.

Crones Don't Whine by Jean Shinoda Bolen

The Millionth Circle by Jean Shinoda Bolen

Goddesses in Everywoman by Jean Shinoda Bolen

Crossing Avalon by Jean Shinoda Bolen

Circles of Stone: Woman's Journey to Herself by Judith Duerk

New and Selected Poems by Mary Oliver

Dare to Be Yourself by Alan Cohen

Why Your Life Sucks and What You Can Do About It by Alan Cohen

The Dragon Doesn't Live Here Anymore by Alan Cohen

The Dance by Oriah Mountain Dreamer

The Call by Oriah Mountain Dreamer

The Invitation by Oriah Mountain Dreamer

Excuse Me, Your Life is Waiting by Lynn Grabhorn

The Dance of the Dissident Daughter by Sue Monk Kidd

The Secret Life of Bees by Sue Monk Kidd

Power vs. Force by David Hawkins

The Power of Full Engagement by Loehr and Schwartz

Fearless Living by Rhonda Britten

Awareness by Anthony De Millo

The Seven Spiritual Laws of Success by Deepak Chopra

The Journey by Brandon Bays

The Velveteen Rabbit by Margery Williams

My Grandfather's Blessings by Rachel Naomi Remen

The Anatomy of the Spirit by Carolyn Myss

Sacred Contracts by Carolyn Myss

Write It Down, Make It Happen by Henriette Anne Klauser

The Right Questions by Debbie Ford

The Secret of the Shadow by Debbie Ford

The Path: Creating Your Mission Statement by Laurie Beth Jones

Inner Work by Robert Johnson

Find Your Purpose, Change Your Life by Carol Adrienne

The Purpose of Your Life by Carol Adrienne

The Path of Transformation by Shakti Gawain

Live in a Better Way by the Dalai Lama

How, Then, Shall We Live? by Wayne Muller

20 Minute Retreats: Revive Your Spirit in Just Minutes by Rachel Harris

The Woman's Retreat Book by Jennifer Louden

The Feeling Good Handbook by David Burns

Soul Mapping: An Imaginative Way to Self Discovery By Frost, Shoup, and Roge

Self Matters: Creating Your Life from the Inside Out by Phil McGraw

When Things Fall Apart by Pema Chodron

Inner Peace for Busy People by Joan Borysenko

Man's Search for Meaning by Victor Frankl

Anything by Wayne Dyer

Writing From the Heart by Nancy Slonim Aronie

Take Time for Your Life by Cheryl Richardson

Stand Up for Your Life by Cheryl Richardson

The Language of Letting Go by Melody Beattie

The Journey to the Heart by Melody Beattie

The Celestine Prophecy by James Redfield

Feel the Fear and Do It Anyway by Susan Jeffers

Wherever You Go, There You Are by Jon Kabat-Zinn

Authentic Happiness by Martin Seligman

A Course in Life by Joan Cuttuso

Return to Love by Marianne Williamson

A Course in Miracles

Loving What Is by Byron Katie

Revolution from Within by Gloria Steinem

Conversations with God by Neale Donald Walsh

To Love and Be Loved by Sam Keen

The Road Less Traveled by M. Scott Peck

Willpower's Not Enough by Washburn & Boundy

The Serenity Prayer Book by William Pietsch

What Happy People Know by Dan Baker

Feelings Buried Alive Never Die by Karol Truman

Coaching with Spirit: Allowing Success to Emerge by Teri-E Belf

Wishcraft by Barbara Sher

Mindfulness-Based Cognitive Therapy by Zindel Segal

Wishing: How to Fulfill Your Heart's Desires by Elizabeth Harper

Visioning by Lucia Capacchione

Soul Sisters by Pythia Peay

Where Two Worlds Touch by Gloria Karpinski

The Power of Now and *The New Earth* by Eckhart Tolle

A Hidden Wholeness by Parker Palmer

Ask and You Will Succeed by Kenneth Foster

The 21-Day Consciousness Cleanse by Debbie Ford

Consider the Possibilities...

WITH AUTHOR KATHY MURPHY, PhD

Kathy Murphy has helped thousands of people achieve profound personal transformation in their lives. By helping you ask and answer powerful questions, Kathy will help you design the life you were always meant to live.

Kathy's programs include:

- *Individual Counseling Sessions*
- *Group Counseling Sessions*
- *Women's Weekend Retreat*
- *Your Possible Life Transformation Program*

Kathy is also available to speak to your audience on topics related to *Your Possible Life*, as well providing training opportunities for other helping professionals to design and facilitate personal growth programs for their clientele.

Kathy's goal is to help you discover your full potential and to be connected with others on the same path. Having a community of like-minded people will enrich your journey of self-discovery in unimaginable ways. Please visit her site to connect to the program that is right for you. www.kathymurphyphd.com

Remember in life all things are possible!

Use this book to motivate, educate, thank, inspire, promote, and connect. We encourage you to give this book as a gift, or keepsake.

Your Possible Life is available in bulk quantities and in customized versions at special discounts for corporate, institutional, and educational purposes. To learn more please contact our Special Sales team at:

1.866.775.1696 · sales@advantageww.com · www.AdvantageSpecialSales.com

Printed in the USA
CPSIA information can be obtained
at www.ICGtesting.com
JSHW012027140824
68134JS00033B/2914